Preface

This book has been some time in the making. About six years ago I was asked to teach a course in the theology and psychology of the person at the Institute for Religious Education and Pastoral Ministry of Boston College. As I began remote preparations for the course, I had in mind a book that would be a theological companion to the book *The Practice of Spiritual Direction* which I had coauthored with William J. Connolly. I approached Brian McDermott, S.J., a friend and former colleague at Weston School of Theology in Cambridge, MA, and asked for some suggestions for reading, especially with reference to the theology of the Trinity. Among other books he recommended John Macmurray's two-volume work *The Form of the Personal.* When I read Macmurray, I became enthralled with the geniality of his approach and realized that I had been looking for such a philosophy of action and of the person for a long time. The students who suffered with me in the struggle to understand and to apply Macmurray's philosophy to theology in the fall of 1986 and of 1987 gave me confidence that we were on to something very helpful for understanding our experience of God and our ministry. I want to thank Brian and these students.

In the course of the next couple of years I published a number of articles in which I used Macmurray to illuminate some issues of interest to me and apparently to others, e.g., the experience of God, the problem of evil, the way God acts in the world, what God's intention for the universe is, the meaning of the Kingdom of God, the discernment of spirits. Some of these articles formed the backbone of the present book, though modified and rearranged to fit my present concerns. I am grateful to the editors and publishers of *America, The Way, The Tablet, Human Development*, and *Review for Religious* not only for publishing my articles, but also for helpful criticism and for allowing me to use the articles in this book. I am also grateful to the many readers who took the time to write to me both to thank me, to share their own experiences with me and to offer critiques.

By the summer of 1989 I had put together five chapters, the first draft of what are now chapters 2, 3, 4, 5 and 6. I showed these to various friends who took the time to read them and to give me detailed comments and encouragement. I am deeply grateful to Mary Guy, O.S.U., Philomena Sheerin, M.M.M., Kathleen M. Barber, Walter J. Conlan, S.J., James W. Bernauer, S.J. and Louis Roy, O.P., for their discerning encouragement and helpful critiques. Walter Conlan paid me the great compliment of translating the draft into Portuguese for use with groups of spiritual directors in Brazil. James M. Keegan, S.J., deserves special commendation; he went over the manuscript with a fine-tooth comb and made many valuable suggestions for making the work more accessible. If it is not more accessible, it is not Jim's fault.

Because of the pressure of other events and work I did nothing further with the manuscript for some time, until I was asked to teach another course at the Institute for Religious Education and Pastoral Ministry in the spring of 1991, by the director of the Institute, Robert Imbelli. I told him about the manuscript, and he enthusiastically recommended that I use it as the basis of a course in the ministry of spiritual discernment. In preparation for that course I did a new draft of the five chapters and added another on the theology of ministry. Once again my students struggled with me as we together tried to grasp the full meaning of Macmurray's thought and its implications for our life of faith and of ministry. In the course of the semester we became a community of friends who worked to help one another to become better ministers of the word and spiritual directors. I am very grateful to Bob Imbelli and to those students.

In the Jesuit Community at Boston College a group of us began to meet to discuss our scholarly work in this "post-

Spiritual Direction and the Encounter with God

A THEOLOGICAL INQUIRY

William A. Barry, S.J.

Paulist Press ✚ New York ✚ Mahwah, N.J.

Scripture taken from the *Holy Bible, New International Version*. Copyright © 1973, 1978, 1984 International Bible Society. Used by permission of Zondervan Bible Publishers.

Portions of chapters 2, 3 and 6 first appeared in *The Way Supplement*. Portions of chapters 3, 4 and 7 first appeared in *Human Development*. Part of chapter 5 first appeared in *Studies in the Spirituality of Jesuits*. Part of chapter 6 first appeared in *Review for Religious* and was part of the Pius Riffel Lecture delivered at Regis College in Toronto. Permission to use these sections is gratefully acknowledged.

Material from *The Self as Agent* and *Persons in Relation* by John Macmurray is reprinted with permission of Humanities Press and of Faber & Faber Ltd. Material from *The Experience of God* by John E. Smith is reprinted with permission of Oxford University Press. Permission is gratefully acknowledged.

Library of Congress Cataloging-in-Publication Data

Barry, William A.
Spiritual direction and the encounter with God : a theological inquiry / William A. Barry.
p. cm.
Includes bibliographical references.
ISBN 0-8091-3305-9
1. Spiritual direction. 2. Spiritual formation—Catholic Church. 3. Catholic Church—Adult education. 4. Experience (Religion) 5. Spiritual directors—Education. I. Title.
BX2350.7.B36 1992
253.5'3—dc20 91-43159
CIP

Published by Paulist Press
997 Macarthur Boulevard
Mahwah, New Jersey 07430

Printed and bound in the
United States of America

Table of Contents

I dedicate this book with affection and gratitude to
John P. Banks, S.J.
John J. Bresnahan, S.J.
Miriam Cleary, O.S.U.
Walter J. Conlan, S.J.
Padraic Leonard, C.S.S.Sp.
Philomena Sheerin, M.M.M.
coworkers, friends and lovers of the Mystery we call God.

modern" world. I presented the central chapters of the manuscript to that group which led to very profitable discussion. I owe thanks to Ronald Anderson, S.J., Joseph Appleyard, S.J., James Bernauer, S.J., Brian Braman, S.J., Edward R. Callahan, S.J., Francis X. Clooney, S.J., David Gill, S.J., Kevin Gillespie, S.J., Roger Haight, S.J., John Haughey, S.J., Charles Healey, S.J., Arthur Madigan, S.J., James Skehan, S.J., William Suchan, S.J., and Ronald Tacelli, S.J. I also take this opportunity to thank the Jesuit Community at Boston College who throughout my three short years as rector were unfailingly supportive and encouraging to me. I want to single out James M. Collins, S.J., and our administrative secretary Cyrilla Mooradian for all the ways they made it possible for me to function and to prosper during those three years.

During the spring semester of 1991 it was announced that I would become the next provincial of the Jesuit province of New England. I knew that I would have difficulty finishing up this book after I became provincial. As a result I sent the manuscript to Donald Brophy, senior editor at Paulist Press, and asked him to give me some strong editorial help so that I could finish it before I was too far into the new job. Don very graciously read the manuscript and to my surprise found it in pretty good shape already. He gave me some helpful pointers for the final rewrite and offered me a contract. I am very grateful to Don for his help and encouragement.

I have dedicated the book to John J. Bresnahan, S.J., and Miriam Cleary, O.S.U., with whom I worked in beginning a training center for spiritual directors in Jamaica, to Miriam and John P. Banks, S.J., with whom I worked in beginning training centers for spiritual directors in Guyana and in Trinidad and Tobago, to Philomena Sheerin, M.M.M., Walter J. Conlan, S.J., and Padraic Leonard, C.S.S.Sp., with whom I worked in the training of spiritual directors in Brazil. They, and the many people in those countries and in the United States who have worked with me, have taught me very much about the varied ways in which we encounter God and by which we help one another to continue to move toward the deepest desire of our hearts, union with the community of the Trinity and with one another.

Finally, I take this opportunity to thank my father, William Barry, my sisters Peg, Mary and Kathleen, and my friend Marika Geoghegan who have been unfailing supporters and discerning readers of my writing. No one becomes a writer without such support. No one becomes a writer without teachers either. I want to thank the Sisters of Mercy who taught me with so much dedication and self-sacrifice at Sacred Heart Grammar School in Worcester, MA, the Xaverian Brothers who helped shape an insecure boy into a relatively self-confident young man at St. John's High School in Worcester, and the Jesuits and their lay colleagues at Holy Cross College, especially the late Fathers Gerard Mears and Harry Bean, who honed my writing skills by creative assignments and hard-nosed, yet caring critiques. In 1950 I entered the Society of Jesus and have been blessed beyond measure by my companionship with many Jesuits throughout the world. Throughout the book there are many indications of my debt to Ignatius of Loyola and his followers. It is a special privilege to finish its writing during the Ignatian Year 1990–1991 celebrating the 500th anniversary of the birth of Ignatius and the 450th anniversary of the founding of the Society of Jesus. *Ad maiorem Dei gloriam!* To the greater glory of God!

July 31, 1991
Feast of St. Ignatius of Loyola
In the 500th year of his birth

O Deus, Ego Amo Te

O God, I love thee, I love thee—
Not out of hope of heaven for me
Nor fearing not to love and be
  In the everlasting burning.
Thou, thou, my Jesus, after me
  Didst reach thine arms out dying,
For my sake sufferedst nails and lance,
Mocked and marrèd countenance,
  Sorrows passing number,
  Sweat and care and cumber,
Yea and death, and this for me,
  And thou couldst see me sinning:
Then I, why should not I love thee,
Jesu so much in love with me?
Not for heaven's sake; not to be
Out of hell by loving thee;
Not for any gains I see;
But just the way that thou didst me
I do love and I will love thee:
What must I love thee, Lord, for then?—
For being my king and God. Amen.

Gerard Manley Hopkins, S.J.

1. Introduction

Spiritual direction has taken on a new and vigorous life in the ministry of the Christian churches since the early 1970s. Centers for training spiritual directors have sprung up all over the world. Perhaps the most popular programs in theological schools and theological departments have to do with spirituality and spiritual direction. Books on spiritual direction have proliferated. A national symposium for spiritual directors and training center staffs had its first two meetings at Mercy Center in Burlingame, California in 1989 and 1990 and its third in Philadelphia at Chestnut Hill College in 1991. Out of the first two symposia arose an organization, Spiritual Directors International, which held its first conference in 1991. Spiritual direction could be described as a growth industry among the ministries of the church.

Throughout the history of the church people have sought the help of other members of the church to nurture their interior life.[1] Such help has taken many forms. Spiritual directors have been seen as fathers or mothers to be obeyed in all things; they have been advisors for organizing one's day around prayer; they have been moral guides and confessors; they have been companions or brothers or sisters on the journey. In our day I have come across instances of each of these kinds of spiritual direction. *The Practice of Spiritual Direction*[2] which I coauthored with William J. Connolly took a particular stance on the purpose of spiritual direction that many have found helpful. It has become a standard textbook in many programs for training spiritual directors and has been translated into several languages. Reviews of the book have generally been favorable. The most perspicacious have, however, made two criticisms that are well-founded. First, the book, they say, focuses too narrowly on prayer experiences as the matter for the conversation between the director and directee. Secondly, they note that the book has an implicit theology which needs explicating. Since, with Fleming,[3] I believe that the practice of spiritual direction needs to become theologically more grounded, I undertake in this book an attempt to respond to both these critiques and thus to make *The Practice* even more helpful to people who are called to this ministry. I also hope that the book can stand on its own and be helpful not only to spiritual directors, but also to many adults interested in deepening their relationship with God and understanding their faith and experience.

In *The Practice of Spiritual Direction* Connolly and I define Christian spiritual direction

> as help given by one Christian to another which enables that person to pay attention to God's personal communication to him or her, to respond to this personally communicating God, to grow in intimacy with this God, and to live out the consequences of the relationship.[4]

In her review of the book Nancy Ring notes that "(w)ith a relentlessness of purpose seldom encountered in any book on any subject" the authors insist "that the purpose of the director is to assist the directee in focusing on the particularity and uniqueness of God's presence to him/her and to become attuned to the dynamics of one's own attraction and resistance to a developing intimacy with God."[5] Such a definition of spiritual direction presupposes that God acts in our world in such a way that we can experience God's action.

Many modern people dismiss such a presupposition out of hand. God, if there be a God, cannot be experienced in this world, they say. In this point of view they find themselves buttressed by many elements of our culture. Analytic philosophy, which has dominated many philosophy departments in the English-speaking world, denies validity to discourse that speaks of the experience of God. Psychologists influenced by Freud and others maintain that "religious experience" is a projection based on childish needs for a benevolent and all-powerful parent. Marx has taught many moderns to look upon religion as the opium of the people. The theory of the sociology of knowledge leads many modern people to consider religion as a product of the culture and society in which people are raised. In fact, much modern philosophy since the critiques of Kant has been caught up in the problem of whether we can know anything real outside ourselves, let alone know the transcendent God.

Moreover, experience itself, quite apart from whether we can have an experience of God, seems problematic to many people. Experience seems by its very nature a purely subjective thing. Yet spiritual direction focuses on experience and expects that people will be able to encounter God there.

Obviously a theology of the spiritual life and of spiritual direction must deal with these questions unless we want to be religious in a ghetto. We must try to give a rationale for our practice that takes into account the questions that surround us almost as the atmosphere does. In the chapters that follow we shall rely on the philosophical work on experience and God by John E. Smith to overcome the bias that looks on experience as purely subjective. We shall also spend a great deal of time with the philosophy of action of the late Scottish philosopher, John Macmurray, because he gives us a way of looking at the modern dilemma and also shows a way out. In the process we shall develop a theory of God's presence in the world that can solidly ground the practice of prayer and of spiritual direction.

The God Christians believe they encounter in this world is not the God of the deists, but the God revealed in Jesus Christ. Our God is one God, but mysteriously three persons. A reviewer of the French edition of *The Practice* notes that we pay little attention to the Trinity in our discussion of the experience of God.[6] An adequate theology of prayer and of spiritual direction must take into account the trinitarian dimension of the encounter with God in this world. Here, too, we will be helped by the philosophy of the person developed by John Macmurray as well as by the work of John O'Donnell on the Trinity. Moreover, we shall also come to see that in spite of the relative isolation of the direction relationship as one-on-one it must be seen as part of the community not only of the Trinity, but also of the church.

Once we have established the rationale for paying attention to experience in order to develop the relationship with God, we are faced with the question of discerning within our experience what is of God from what is not of God. We can delude ourselves about our experience of God. In the history of spirituality people have always seen the need for testing experience. Within the Ignatian tradition such testing has been called the discernment of spirits. A theology of the spiritual life and of spiritual direction must be able to account for such discernment. The groundwork laid in the previous chapters will help us to point out a pattern in the development of the relationship with God and show the necessity of discernment and the criteria by which discernment is made. Here modern psychology will be drawn on to develop our theology.

As a form of pastoral counseling spiritual direction necessarily focuses on the experience of the individual. Such a focus can lead and, indeed, has led to the development of an individualistic spirituality. Moreover, because spiritual direction, like many of the modern "talking" therapies, has developed among the relatively well-educated, it has seemed removed from the cares and concerns of ordinary people. In fact, the tendency of much modern pastoral and psychological counseling has been to concentrate on those who are the more privileged members of society. In a world where more and more people are aware of our interdependence on one another and of the serious inequities brought on by individualism, and within the context of the church's call for a faith and spirituality that also practices justice, an adequate theology of the spiritual life and of spiritual direction will have to show how it fits into this larger picture of the ministry of the church.

Finally, spiritual direction is a ministry within the church. Historically this ministry has not been limited to those who are ordained. What are the theological grounds for the ministry of spiritual direction and how can it be grounded ecclesially? I hope we will be able to answer these questions adequately as the argument progresses.

In the preface to the published version of his Gifford Lectures, of which more will be said in subsequent chapters, John Macmurray gave a pithy summary of his argument in the two volumes. "All meaningful knowledge is for the sake of action, and all meaningful action is for the sake of friendship."[7] In other words, thought that has no relation to action is pure speculation which cannot be verified in action and is, therefore, meaningless. But meaningful action, his argument holds, must ultimately intend the fostering of community, or friendship. If I may be so bold, let me try to summarize the argument of this book in an analogous fashion though not in so pithy a form. Reflection on our experience reveals the mysterious presence of God who is always acting to draw us into community with the Trinity and thus with one another; this community is the Kingdom of God and its bond is the Holy Spirit poured out into our hearts. Fear and egocentrism lead us to resist God's action, and spiritual direction is a singularly appropriate ministry to help us to overcome our fears.

The ultimate aim of all ministry in the church, but especially of the ministry of spiritual direction, is to help people come to the point where they can say and mean the favorite prayer of St. Francis Xavier, "O Deus, ego amo te," which appeared in the beginning of this book in the poetic translation of Hopkins. Anyone who can pray this prayer will, like Xavier, be a person for others. Finally, as we begin this study, may I suggest that we make our own the prayer of Anselm of Canterbury in the first chapter of his *Proslogion* (modified from the first person singular to the first person plural).

> Teach us to seek You, and reveal Yourself to us as we seek; for unless You instruct us we cannot seek You, and unless You reveal Yourself we cannot find You. Let us seek You in desiring You; let us desire You in seeking You. Let us find You in loving You; let us love you in finding You.[8]

2. Understanding God's Presence in the World

The spiritual life and the practice of spiritual direction assume that God acts in the world and can be experienced in the world. Indeed, Judeo-Christian faith affirms that God, the creator of the universe, acts in this world. God walks with Adam and Eve in the garden in the cool of the day (Gen 3:8). God tells Abram to leave his own land and go into a land which God will show him (Gen 12:1). The whole Abraham cycle of stories beginning with chapter 12 of the Book of Genesis tells of a growing intimacy between God and Abraham.[1] God speaks to Moses and to the prophets. In the New Testament God's voice is heard at the baptism (Lk 3:22) and transfiguration of Jesus (Lk 9:35). The risen Jesus appears to the Eleven and others (Lk 24:36–49) and finally, long after the Ascension, to Paul on the road to Damascus (Acts 9:3–6). Throughout history, and even in our own day, people have affirmed that they have experienced the presence of God both in communal and personal prayer.[2] Such assertions, we noted, are problematic to many modern people, so much so that even believers can wonder about their validity. We need to develop a theory that makes our faith assertions plausible. In this chapter I want to propose a way of arriving at a dim and analogous understanding of God's presence in our world. In the next I shall propose a way of understanding experience that makes it plausible to put the focus of spiritual direction on experience.

Can We Know Ourselves and Our World?

Anyone familiar with modern philosophy knows that it has been grappling with the question of how we can be sure of our knowledge of reality. In his *Critique of Pure Reason* Emmanuel Kant set the problem by showing rather convincingly that we can only know the phenomenal world, the world of our experience, but have no way of knowing by reason whether this phenomenal world corresponds to the real world. John Macmurray, the Scottish philosopher who died in 1976, came to the conclusion that modern philosophy had started down a blind alley when it accepted Descartes' dictum, "I think, therefore I am," as the foundation stone for the knowledge of reality and thus of any system of philosophy. With such a starting point Kant's critique is virtually unassailable.

In his Gifford lectures of 1953–54[3] Macmurray demonstrates that starting down this blind alley leads to a dead end. In philosophy itself the dead end is agnosticism or atheism. If my primary knowledge is of myself as thinker, then I have no immediate knowledge of anything outside myself. I have to argue to the existence of the outside world, and any argument one uses, as Kant has shown, is problematic. If the very existence of a world outside myself is problematic, the existence of God is even more problematic. Agnosticism and atheism are close to hand.

> The reason is that the adoption of the "I think" as the centre of reference and starting-point of his philosophy makes it formally impossible to do justice to religious experience. For thought is inherently private; and any philosophy which takes its stand on the primacy of thought, which defines the Self as the Thinker, is committed formally to an extreme logical individualism. It is necessarily egocentric.[4]

In the political realm Macmurray argues that the dead end is totalitarian government, but we need not go into that argument.

We Know Ourselves and Our World in Action

As an alternative to the Cartesian starting-point Macmurray proposes that philosophy begin with what is primary in our experience; we are not primarily thinkers, we are doers, but knowing doers, that is, agents. Thus, philosophy begins with the "I do" rather than with the "I think." Action includes knowledge: "To do, and to know that I do, are two aspects of one and the same experience. *This* knowledge is absolute and necessary. It is not, however, knowledge of an object but what we may call 'knowledge in action,' "[5] i.e., the unreflective, primary knowledge of any experience of action. When I act, I know that I am acting and what I intend. Action is, therefore, the actualizing of a possibility, the determining of a future. Hence, the possibility of action implies free will. "To deny free-will is to deny the possibility of action. . . . That I am free is an immediate implication of the 'I do'; and to deny freedom is to assert that no one ever *does* anything, that no one is capable even of thinking or observing."[6] What is actualized when I act is the past, and as such (i.e., as past) completely determined. In other words, the past cannot be undone; I am not free with regard to the past. But the future, precisely as future, is not yet determined; it is something to be determined by action. Thus, the condition of possibility for action is my freedom.

Action and Event

Macmurray distinguishes an event from an action. An event is simply what happens. A hurricane, for example, or an automobile accident are events. The writing of this chapter is an action. Every event has a cause; every action has a reason. Events are attributed to non-agents; acts to agents, in other words, to persons. One does not ask what a hurricane intended, although people do ask whether the hurricane was an action of God, i.e., whether it was intended by God to punish evildoers.

An interesting example of the difference between an event and an action is provided by Ignatius of Loyola in his *Autobiography.* He was on his way from Loyola, where he had recovered from battle wounds, to Montserrat. During his recovery he was converted from a worldly life and had begun to learn the discernment of spirits. The story indicates, however, that Ignatius was still far from being a mature discerner of spirits. On the road he met a Moor, and in the course of their conversation the Moor made a comment about Our Lady that bothered Ignatius. The Moor, perhaps sensing the rising tension, went on ahead rapidly. Ignatius, on his mule, began to puzzle over what he should do. Should he go after the Moor and strike him with his sword to preserve Mary's honor? Or should he let him go? Ignatius writes:

> Tired of examining what would be best to do and not finding any guiding principle, he decided as follows, to let the mule go with the reins slack as far as the place where the road separated. If the mule took the village road, he would seek out the Moor and strike him; if the mule did not go toward the village but kept on the highway, he would let him go. . . . Our Lord willed that the mule took the highway and not the village road.[7]

Obviously the mule did not have the intention of saving the Moor; so we presume that the activity of the mule was an event. But Ignatius attributes intention to God; so for Ignatius the whole activity is an action of God which includes the actions of Ignatius in letting the reins go free and the event of the mule's following the highway.

All actions include events as part of their constitution. For example, I write a letter to a friend. This action includes within it habits such as my style of handwriting and the involuntary muscular and other physiological events which are essential to my act of writing, but not what I deliberately intend.

When I act, I know that I exist and I also know that what is not-I (which Macmurray calls "the Other") exists. I do not have to reason to the knowledge of my own and the world's existence. When I shake your hand, for example, I am absolutely certain (I know) that you and I exist. In action I encounter you. In the next chapter we shall take up a definition of experience as encounter that dovetails nicely with this insight of Macmurray. For present purposes I merely want to add that this philosophy of action also leads to the surprising conclusion that the primary sense is not sight, but touch. At all times I am in touch with the Other since I am supported by the forces of gravity, the ground upon which I stand or the chair upon which I sit. Touch is the primary sense by which I encounter the Other.

Understanding the Person: The "Form of the Personal"

Macmurray argues that a philosophy of the person must not use the impersonal as its explanatory tool. Yet all explanations of the personal that use analogies from the physical or biological world make this mistake. If, for example, the human person is compared to a biological organism, then the explanation uses the pattern of development of the organic as thesis, antithesis, synthesis. Organisms develop in this pattern. Erikson's stage theory of personality development is a perfect example of this pattern.[8] The successful completion of one stage (synthesis) leads to a new step in development (thesis) which provokes a crisis (antithesis) leading to a new synthesis. Thus, the successful completion of Erikson's first stage results in a sense of basic trust in the child. This trust leads the child to want to try out her new skills, to do things her own way. But the child soon finds out that she cannot do whatever she wants. For example, she cannot do what she wants for lack of skills; or she is forbidden by her parents to do some things she wants to do. Out of the crisis of this collision of thesis and antithesis, if all works well, comes the sense of relative autonomy which Erikson believes is the best outcome of the second stage. But notice that this explanation of personal development leaves no room for freedom. The process is automatic, even though it does allow for interaction between the organism and the environment such that the outcome is not sure at the beginning. Macmurray believes that the personal must be explained on its own grounds. A new pattern must be discovered by reflection on human activity itself. This pattern he calls the "form of the personal."

Instead of discovering a dialectical pattern as the form of the personal, reflection on human action finds a pattern in which a positive includes and is constituted by its own negative. This is an abstract and difficult concept to grasp. Let me illustrate it by a couple of examples. We have already noted the distinction between action and event. Take action as the positive. Any action is intentional. An event, on the contrary, is not intentional; it just happens. Thus event is the negative of action. Yet no action can occur in the absence of events because any action includes events (e.g., muscular contractions, molecular activity). But since without these events no action would take place, any action is constituted by these events. Thus any action includes and is constituted by events, the negative of action. Another example comes from the dichotomy between thought and action. Again action is the positive, since thought is defined as the negative of action. When I am just thinking, I withdraw from action. But when I act, I am also thinking. In fact, without thought I cannot act since action is defined as intentional. As I act, I know what I intend to do. Thus, any action (the positive) includes and is constituted by thought (the negative).

The World As One Action

At the end of the first series of Gifford lectures Macmurray argues that from the standpoint of the "I do" the only coherent way to think of the world is as one action.[9] Overly simplified, his argument runs in this fashion. First of all, to act at all I need to count on the world outside me. But if the world is not a unity in some manner, then I could not count on it to assist me in my actions. Hence, I could not act. Thus, the real world must constitute a unity since it is beyond doubt that I act. Now this unity can be either a unity of process, i.e., a unified series of events, or a unity of action. If the world is one process, then there are no actions, including our own. All such "actions" are part of the one process which is determined, i.e., in a real sense "over and done with"—which would make freedom and intentionality illusory. But I cannot deny the fact that I act. Thus, it is not possible to think the world as one process. On the other hand, because action includes and is constituted by events, it is possible to think the world as one action, informed by a unitary intention. Macmurray then goes on to argue that in order to act we must regard the world as a unity of action because our action requires the cooperation of the world of which we are a part. He says:

> If we could not rely upon the world outside us, we could not act in it. We can act only through knowledge of the Other (he means, what is not "I"); and only what is a determinable unity can be known. It does not follow . . . that its future can be completely determined in advance; only that whatever occurs must be systematically related to what has gone before, so that through all its changes the world remains one world.[10]

How can such a thought be verified? Macmurray argues that the possibility of verification resides in the effect it has on intention and action.

> If we act as if the world, in its unity, is intentional; that is, if we believe in practice that the world is one action . . . we shall act differently from anyone who does not believe this. We shall act as though our own actions were our contributions to the one inclusive action which is the history of the world. . . . Our conception of the unity of the world determines a way of life; and the satisfactoriness or unsatisfactoriness of that way of life is its verification.[11]

Such a line of reasoning obviously tends toward the affirmation of a God who is the universal agent.[12]

At the end of the second series of Gifford Lectures Macmurray returns to this issue, only now he entitles his last chapter "The Personal Universe." Here he makes explicit what was only implicit at the end of the first series. The following paragraph sums up his argument:

> There is, then, only one way in which we can think our relation to the world, and that is to think it as a personal

> relation, through the form of the personal. We must think that the world is one action, and that its impersonal aspect is the negative aspect of this unity of action, contained in it, subordinated within it, and necessary to its constitution. To conceive the world thus is to conceive it as the act of God, the Creator of the world, and ourselves as created agents, with a limited and dependent freedom to determine the future, which can be realized only on the condition that our intentions are in harmony with His intention, and which must frustrate itself if they are not.[13]

An Example of One Action

It may help to understand what Macmurray is saying to consider an extended example from ordinary human experience. I decided to write this book. My intention was to explain Macmurray in such a way that others would have an insight which would affect their life and ministry. This one action, whose intention was to have an effect on others, included a number of other actions. For instance, I read and reread Macmurray with the intention of understanding him, and I wrote several drafts of the book and the final draft. It also included a manifold of events, happenings that were not actions since I did not intend them, e.g., eye-hand coordination in writing and typing, writing skills, memories and associations. Moreover, as I wrote I became aware of new questions—puzzles that I had not thought of before—and my action had to be adjusted accordingly. To complicate the issue even further my action depends on the action of others. I must convince an editor to publish my book and must hope that at least some readers will read it. The success of my intention depends, in other words, on other free agents as well as on many events, such as the safe delivery of the mail.

In this extended example the one action I intend is the publication of this book with the hope that others will read it. It is one action because it has one intention. It is personal because it is my action. My one action is done when I am satisfied that I have done all that I can to attain my intention. The great thrill and challenge of being human is acting in a complex world, committing ourselves to an action that is long-term and requires the cooperation of other agents. For example, the life-project of a marriage can be seen as the one action of each of the spouses which is only completed when one of them dies. This one action includes many other actions and millions of events. The glory of being a human being is that we can act in such a way. Why not use such an analogy to understand in some dim fashion God's relation to the universe rather than analogies from the physical and biological sciences?[14]

God's Intention for God's One Action

If we understand the world as one action of God, we mean that God has a unitary intention for the whole creation and that his one action includes and is constituted by all the actions of every created agent and all the events that will ever occur in the history of the universe. In other words, the one action of God includes the free actions of all of us human beings. Because we really are agents, the future of God's action is not determined, since only the past is completely determined. So in some mysterious way God's action depends on us. Our faith tells us that God's intention will not ultimately be thwarted—as my intention in writing this book may be thwarted both by my own inadequacy and by the actions of other agents. At the same time our faith and our experience tell us that we really are free agents, not pawns in the great chess game of creation. If our actions are truly free, then, again in some mysterious fashion, God's one action includes them and adjusts to them in order to attain God's intention.

Ignatius of Loyola tells us in his autobiography that he was determined to live and die in Jerusalem when he went there as a pilgrim after his time in Manresa. The provincial of the Franciscans in charge of the holy places in Jerusalem ordered him to leave with the rest of the pilgrims and threatened him with excommunication if he did not obey.[15] Ignatius could have decided to risk excommunication and to stay in Jerusalem, in which case the Society of Jesus would not have been founded and world history would have been different. God's one action would have had to take this act of Ignatius into account. Does such a conception of God's one action limit God? It seems to me that God's immensity is immeasurably enhanced if we understand God as one who can attain God's one intention for the world when the one action includes free choices by human agents which seem inimical to God's intention.

In other words, we reflect on our greatest gift, that which makes us humans at all, namely, our capacity for action, and apply it analogously to God. If we knew the future, it would already be determined; hence, we would not be free. It is not an imperfection not to know the future; it is the condition of freedom. Free action is precisely the determination of the future. The result of action is history, the past which cannot be undone, and which is, therefore, wholly determined and knowable. Given this line of argument, the dogma of God's sovereign freedom must mean that God, too, in some analogous fashion only knows the future as God acts to determine it, in other words, as God's present. Here, too, the analogy limps badly because God is not time-bound as we are. God simultaneously in his eternal present knows the future as he creates it.

In *A Brief History of Time: From the Big Bang to Black Holes,* Stephen Hawking begins his concluding chapter:

> We find ourselves in a bewildering world. We want to make sense of what we see around us and to ask: What is the nature of the universe? What is our place in it and where did it and we come from? Why is it the way it is?[16]

He then proceeds to argue that scientists are very close to a unified theory of the universe.

> Up to now, most scientists have been too occupied with the development of new theories that describe *what* the universe is to ask the question *why.* On the other hand, the people whose business it is to ask *why,* the philoso-

> phers, have not been able to keep up with the advance of scientific theories.[17]

He then goes on to say:

> However, if we do discover a complete theory, it should in time be understandable in broad principle by everyone, not just a few scientists. Then we shall all, philosophers, scientists, and just ordinary people, be able to take part in the discussion of the question why it is that we and the universe exist. If we find the answer to that, it would be the ultimate triumph of human reason—for then we would know the mind of God.[18]

Even then, however, we would need revelation to know the intention of the universal Agent, the Mystery we name God.

The human analogy may help us here. No one can really know the intention of another's action unless the other reveals it. I may try to deduce your intention from your behavior, but such deductions are at best based on circumstantial evidence and, therefore, always hypothetical. As Macmurray says: "All knowledge of persons is by revelation."[19] If this is true of human beings, how much more true of God. So the question is: has God revealed God's intention for the universe? At the least, Christians believe, God has revealed the intention for our world, whatever may be said of the whole universe. God's intention, it seems, is that all human beings live as brothers and sisters in a community of faith, hope and love united with Jesus Christ as sons and daughters of God, our Father, and in harmony with the whole created universe.

> Blessed be the God and Father of our Lord Jesus Christ. . . . For he has made known to us in all wisdom and insight the mystery of his will, according to his purpose which he set forth in Christ as a plan for the fullness of time, to unite all things in him, things in heaven and things on earth (Eph 1:3, 9–10).

God's one action will be attained—because God is God. How those who willfully refuse to be brought into the one community of God's family are included in God's one action is not for us to know. What we do know, in faith, is that no created being is excluded from the one action which is this world.

In another context I have argued that the Kingdom of God preached by Jesus can be understood as God's one action. The Kingdom as preached by Jesus is transcendent (not of this world) and yet immanent, not yet present but present, found in community but not identified with any present community, not even the Catholic Church. We can understand the Kingdom of God as God's intention for the universe, or rather as God's one action which is the universe.[20]

Conclusion

We began this chapter with the question of how we might understand in some dim fashion God's presence in the world. We have argued with Macmurray that God is present in the one action which is the universe in an analogous manner to the way we are present in our actions. God is transcendent; God is not the world, just as we are not our actions. Yet God is immanent in the one action because God is doing it just as, analogously, we are immanent in our actions as we do them. Thus, we have plausible grounds for our faith that we do encounter God in this universe.

3. The Religious Dimension of Experience

With Macmurray's concept of action we have come, I believe, to a dim, analogous understanding of God's presence in the world. God is present because the world is God's action. We still have not yet come to grips with the question of how we experience God's action in our world. In the examples with which we began the last chapter people were said to have spoken with God, to have heard God. How are we to understand such language?

Difficulties with the Concept "Religious Experience"

In *The Practice of Spiritual Direction* Connolly and I speak often of religious experience as the focus of the direction sessions. We assumed, with the whole of the Christian spiritual tradition, that God could be experienced, but we did not try to articulate a theological understanding of how God is experienced. Moreover, we believed that the words "religious experience" were relatively straightforward and unambiguous. In time, however, I became more and more uncomfortable with the term "religious experience." The term can tempt readers to consider religious experience something esoteric, mystical, out of the ordinary, something reserved to "holy" people. And in some circles the term conjures up images of the mystical, the supernatural, the ecstatic, the quite frankly strange. William James' use of examples in his classic *The Varieties of Religious Experience*[1] has set the tone in the psychology of religion for understanding the term "religious experience" in this way, even if he is careful to note that he is using the spectacular because it is more illuminating, not because "religious experience" refers only to such extraordinary phenomena. Not so careful is Walter H. Clark[2] who in effect equates religious experience with the ecstatic and mystical and speaks about using LSD to induce such states. If religious experience is equated with such special states, many will doubt that they have any religious experience, and directors will shy away from asking about religious experience or discussing it.

The Religious Dimension of Experience

Along with the insights of Macmurray the work of the American philosopher, John E. Smith, has given me a new slant on the question of the experience of God. *In Experience and God*[3] Smith speaks of the religious dimension of experience rather than of religious experience. For the believer, he concludes, any human experience can have a religious dimension, can be an encounter with God. Reflection on Smith's argument will, I believe, help us to to broaden our view of what can be included under the label "religious experience" and lessen some of our fears of the reality. In the process we will also come to a better understanding of the phrases "finding God in all things" and "being a contemplative in action," phrases so distinctive of Ignatian spirituality.

Experience as Encounter

Smith's first step recovers the concept "experience" from being trapped in the realm of the purely subjective. He maintains that the chief error in defining experience as subjective or "mental" lies in "the uncritical assumption that experience is a record or report to be found entirely within the mind, consciousness, or feeling of an individual being." Such an assumption leads to the contrast between what is "in the mind" and what is "outside" or "objective." He, then, continues:

> If, instead of thus prejudicing the nature of experience at the outset, experience were to be understood as a product of the intersection of something encountered and a being capable of having the encounter, apprehending it, and feeling itself in the encounter, and capable of interpreting the results, the need to assign the labels "subjective" and "objective" uniquely to one side or the other would vanish.[4]

Because of the uncritical assumption so prevalent in our culture, most of us do not trust experience, and have the feeling that there is some objective litmus test of what is true or false, valid or invalid. One of the more common forms of prejudice against women, for example, is the assertion that "they are too subjective; they rely too much on experience and intuition." The uncritical assumption derives from the same Cartesian roots that Macmurray decries as the source of the dualism that both pervades our culture and threatens to destroy it.[5] I do not know whether Macmurray knew of American pragmatism, but at this point he and Smith dovetail nicely. When I shake your hand, I encounter you.

The Mutuality of the Encounter

Thus, experience is the product of a complex encounter between "what exists" and a being with consciousness. Both beings have structures that condition the nature of the experience. Moreover, "as a product, experience is a result of an ongoing process that takes time and has a temporal structure."[6] Experiences are not episodic, nor unrelated. My experience of seeing a tree, for example, involves an encounter with a real tree at a particular season of the year, my past experiences with trees, my state of mind and feeling this time, and so forth. I am not a passive *tabula rasa* upon which the external world impinges. I am actively engaged in making sense of what I encounter. My world would be nothing but a confusion of discrete sense impressions if I did not organize them into a coherent pattern, and the organizing capacity is the result not only of innate structure, but also of what I have learned over my lifetime. Think of the difference between the experience we amateurs have when we hear Beethoven's Seventh Symphony, and that of a celebrated conductor. Both of us "hear" the same music being played, but our experience is vastly different because of our past histories, training, and talent for music. At the same time we amateurs may have very different experiences of Beethoven's Seventh at a concert by the Boston Symphony Orchestra directed by Seiji Ozawa, and at a concert by a college symphony orchestra even though both orchestras play all the notes correctly as Beethoven wrote them. Thus, as Smith says, experience is the product of a complex encounter.

Experience in this sense can, I believe, be equated with one of the ways Lonergan uses the word consciousness.[7] My operations of seeing, hearing, tasting, inquiring, judging, deciding, and expressing attend to an object and are conscious operations of a subject. In Smith's terms: I encounter an object and I am at the same time conscious both of the object and of my own operations. Experience thus includes all that I am conscious of now, where "now" is a temporal process, not a succession of unconnected instants. My experience depends both on the being which is encountered and on my own past history, my learned categories of apperception, my desires, my purposes, my hopes and dreams. The English theologian Martin Thornton makes the same point in a charming image:

> A rose, then, is by selection and interpretation, something different to different people. To the botanist it is *rosaceae arvensis*, to the gardener it is an Ena Harkness, to the aesthete a beautiful sight, and to the blind man it is a wonderful smell. . . . None of these have experienced the rose in its totality, but when Temple's religious man says that it is a creature of God which may disclose his presence, his interpretation is no less valid.[8]

Before I move on to take up the notion of the religious dimension of experience, I want to underline the importance of the insights suggested by Smith. There is no human experience that is not an encounter. Human beings are part and parcel of the reality of this universe. Even the most "subjective" experience, for example, an hallucination, happens to a person who is encountering the air, the ground, the forces of gravity, etc., of the universe, and these "objective" elements impinge on and condition the experience. Moreover, the most "objective" experience, for example, the experience of a scientist recording movements on a dial, depends on the expectations, the beliefs, the paradigm which the scientist assumes. If the scientist does not expect to see a new star, he does not "see" it; whatever else his experience is, it is not the experience of a new star.[9] Nor is there any reason to assume that the paradigms of the scientist or the expectations and desires and illusions of an ordinary citizen are not part of the universe and, therefore, as "objective" as a table or an atom. After all, these so-called "subjective" factors affect human action in the universe and thus have an effect on and in the universe.[10]

The Dimensions of Experience

Any human experience, therefore, as the product of an encounter within the universe, has many dimensions. There is a physical dimension because we are physical beings in a physical universe. There is a biological dimension because we are biological beings in a biological universe. There are psychological and sociological dimensions because we approach any experience as a product of our psychological and sociological histories in the universe. We are not always aware of these dimensions of our experience, but they condition the experience nonetheless. For the person who is not aware of nor attentive to a particular dimension the experience does not have that dimension. Of course, we may have to go to some lengths to "explain" parts of our experience. For example, a man who is not aware of the psychological dimension of experience may hear a noise rustling in the leaves beside the road on a dark night, look around in fright and "see something moving." He shrieks in terror: "I've seen a ghost and it's after me." For this person the ghost is real, not a product of imagination and projection. Later on when his friends scoff at him, he may have to engage in elaborate arguments to prove the existence of the ghost. But he may become convinced by their questions that he was mistaken. Then by reflection he can become aware of the psychological dimension of his experience. Thus, by reflection we can turn our attention to one or the other of these dimensions, and in this way become aware of them. The man who "saw" the ghost may, for example, have doubts about the reality of the ghost and then ponder on how he could have come to such a belief. Such reflection, when it becomes disciplined and aims at universal explanation, leads to one of the empirical sciences. Such reflection, when it becomes disciplined and aims at the creation of a particular work, leads to one of the arts.

The Religious Dimension of Experience

Is there a religious dimension to human experience? If experience is encounter, the answer to this question turns on whether there is a God who is actually encountered, i.e., who is immanent in (as well as transcendent to) this universe and on whether the person who encounters this God expects to encounter God, i.e., is on the alert for God. The religious dimension of human experience is supplied by the believing and seeking person *and* by the Mystery encountered. For Christian believers any experience can have a religious dimension because they believe that God is not only transcendent to but also immanent in his created universe.

Macmurray, as we have seen, argues that the only coherent way to think our relation to the world is to think that the world is one action informed by one intention.

> To conceive the world thus is to conceive it as the act of God, the Creator of the world, and ourselves as created agents, with a limited and dependent freedom to determine the future, which can be realized only on the condition that our intentions are in harmony with His intention, and which must frustrate itself if they are not.[11]

In other words, according to Macmurray, any action of ours occurs within a universe which is one action of God. Hence, at every moment every human being encounters the creator God whose action the universe is. Whether we know it or not, God is ingredient in every human experience. This insight grounds, I believe, a somewhat enigmatic statement by Smith. While underscoring the notion that experience is encounter he says: "Experience is at the very least a dyadic affair and it is even possible that it is irreducibly triadic in character. . . ."[12] Given everything else that Smith says, I take the latter phrase to mean what I have just indicated. Every human experience can, therefore, have a religious dimension for a believer who expects to encounter God.

It may seem strange to speak of encountering or experiencing God. How can we experience the totally Other? Is there not a total incompatibility between revelation and the approach to God through experience? Smith argues that those who hold for such an incompatibility believe

> that revelation is a special way of knowing that is utterly different from, and wholly discontinuous with, human understanding as it comes into play on occasions when our concern is not with God but with other persons and things in the world. Revelation in the religious sense does involve something out of the ordinary, but it is unlikely that the manifestation of God would be intelligible to us at all if it happened only at times when man's capacities for experience and understanding are totally suspended. It is more likely that revelation would require, especially for its reception by the human mind, not the suspension of human capabilities, but rather their participation in an intensified form. Those who have interpreted revelation as a totally alien intervention into history, a message that falls into man's lap, as it were, from the outside, have usually been motivated by a desire to protect the divine mystery from the claims of an irreverent gnosticism. This aim is not without validity, but it can be accomplished in a way that is not self-defeating. Whatever is totally

> different from all we can experience and apprehend must be something that we neither experience nor apprehend and, far from calling this God, we should rather call it nothing at all.[13]

Faith and experience mutually reinforce one another. If I did not believe in God, I would not experience him, although I might have to engage in some rationalizations to explain away some of my experiences. But because I believe in God, I discover in my experience more than what at first blush seemed to be there and name that "more" God. The experience reinforces my belief. Karl Rahner makes this point about the experience of resurrection:

> Naturally, the situation is not such that we first have the experience: Aha, everything is going just fine!—so that we are then led to believe. Instead, somehow or other this faith and this experience mutually determine each other. Only the believer can have this experience—and because he has it, he believes.[14]

In other words, the believer encounters God and knows God prior to any reflection on the experience and prior to "really" knowing what has been experienced. The disciples on the road to Emmaus felt their hearts burning even before they "knew" Jesus in the breaking of the bread. When they came to believe, then they knew what they had experienced; and the reflected experience reinforced their belief.

An Example of the Multidimensionality of Experience

In *Sacred Journey* Frederick Buechner provides a wonderful example of an experience which had many dimensions, including for him a religious dimension. After his father's tragic suicide his mother took him and his brother to Bermuda where they stayed for two years. At thirteen, near the end of his stay, he was sitting with a girl of thirteen on a wall watching ferries come and go. Quite innocently, he says,

> our bare knees happened to touch for a moment, and in that moment I was filled with such a sweet panic and anguish of longing for I had no idea what that I knew my life could never be complete until I found it. . . . It was the upward- reaching and fathomlessly hungering, heart-breaking love for the beauty of the world at its most beautiful, and, beyond that, for that beauty east of the sun and west of the moon which is past the reach of all but our most desperate desiring and is finally the beauty of Beauty itself, of Being itself and what lies at the heart of Being.[15]

Buechner himself notes that there are many ways of looking at this experience. It was just a chance occurrence heightened by his own fragility and the time of day, some might say. Others might attribute the experience to his need to find a father to replace the one he lost so tragically, and so he interpreted his experience as a gift of God. Others might just say that in teenagers the awakening of sexual drives are often interpreted religiously. Buechner agrees with each of these interpretations and thus acknowledges that the experience is multidimensional. He goes on to say that

> looking back at those distant years I choose not to deny, either, the compelling sense of an unseen giver and a series of hidden gifts as not only another part of their reality, but the deepest part of all.[16]

Thus, he finds a religious dimension to his experience. I might add that his experience as a thirteen-year-old is much like the experience C. S. Lewis called Joy.[17]

The Mediation of the Encounter with God

Smith goes on to argue that the revelation of God occurs through an historical medium. Hence, in human experience God is directly encountered, but mediately, not immediately.[18] Without referring to sacramental theology Smith touches on the sacramental nature of reality when he says: "For Christianity every disclosure of God is also a disclosure of something else at the same time."[19]

Traditionally the central media of God's self-disclosure have been the holy or prophetic person, historical occasions, nature, and scripture. For the Christian the historical medium *par excellence* is Jesus Christ who reveals that God is most centrally self-sacrificing love. When we encounter Jesus, we also encounter God, and God reveals that God's essence is self-sacrificing love.

Before we pass too quickly to the traditional religious media of God's presence, I want to emphasize that any human experience, hence any medium, can disclose God. It may tax our ingenuity to discern the presence of God in some experiences, but the difficulty should not blind us to the truth our faith teaches us. For example, a scrupulous person has an image of God as a tyrant who wants exact obedience to minute laws. If such a person should come to the point where she curses this God who makes life hell, it may well be that the drive to curse this God comes from the Spirit of God who cannot abide idols. The Dutch Jewess, Etty Hillesum, found God through a rather flawed psychotherapist and in the midst of the horrors of the Nazi roundup of Jews in Amsterdam.[20]

Thus, we have the theological and philosophical grounds for the kataphatic tradition of prayer which advocates the use of the contemplation of nature and the imaginative reading and contemplation of scripture. This tradition, often associated with Ignatius of Loyola, but not limited to him, underlies much of the discussion of the experience of God in *The Practice of Spiritual Direction*. My own belief is that the apophatic tradition of imageless prayer, exemplified by the work of John Main and Basil Pennington,[21] cannot avoid some mediation of the experience of the Mystery we call God. Perhaps the difference in the two traditions lies in the desire of the apophatic tradition to bypass the other dimensions to get to the heart of Mystery, and that of the kataphatic to try to discern the religious dimension within the other dimensions. In any case both methods of prayer aim at helping people to encounter the living God.

As noted earlier, when we encounter God through some

historical medium, we do so not as a *tabula rasa*. The experience is colored, not only by the nature of the medium, but also by all that we are at the time of the encounter as well as by the conditions of the environment in which we live and move and have our being. Thus the weather, atmospheric conditions, the state of one's health, one's state of mind, one's preoccupations, desires, expectations, whether one is alone or with others—all these influences and many more have a bearing on the experience. The very same experience that has a religious dimension has physical, biological, psychological, sociological and cultural dimensions as well. Precisely because the encounter with God is multidimensional, Christians have always been cautioned to be discerning. Discernment is necessary not only because of the possible influence of the evil spirit, but also because of the multidimensionality of human experience. It is also helpful to realize that every experience I have depends on my prior expectations. I experience nothing without having assimilated it to schemata or structures built up over my history.[22] All experience is partly a construction of the one who experiences. So both the believer and the nonbeliever approach life and the question of God with constructs. Neither has the advantage of being more "objective" or "realistic" or "rational."[23] Moreover, belief in a God who discloses himself can be grounded by recourse to reflection on our experience. So to approach life as a believer need not be illusory.

Focusing the Theological Question

When we speak of experiencing God, we use concrete, interpersonal language. We say things like this: "I felt as though God held me in his arms;" "God seemed like a light surrounding me;" "God said that he loved me." The mythological language which we must use in order to talk at all about God makes it seem that God intervenes into the world to communicate with us. The tendency is to think of God as acting in the world from outside it. Many of our petitionary prayers, for example, ask God to do something to change our situation. We pray for rain during drought, for the healing of sick relatives, for a safe trip. In personal and communual prayer we ask God to make himself known to us, to let us know that he loves us as he loved Israel. And we take certain experiences as answers to our prayers. How are we to make theological sense of these faith experiences?

An Example from the Life of Jesus

For the sake of an example, let us presume that the experience of the voice of God described in Mark's account of Jesus' baptism was an experience that Jesus alone had. "As Jesus was coming up out of the water, he saw heaven being torn open and the Spirit descending on him like a dove. And a voice came from heaven: 'You are my Son, whom I love; with you I am well pleased' " (Mk 1:10–11). In spiritual direction, often enough, directees describe experiences in such imaginative terms. Can we get some understanding of God's action in this experience from the philosophical ideas of Macmurray and Smith, an understanding, by the way, that not only does not denigrate the mythological language used, but even makes such language appropriate and necessary?

First, let's return to the example used earlier to illuminate Macmurray's concept of one action, namely, my one action of writing and publishing this book. As readers come to grips with the book, they encounter not only the printed page, but also me, or at least my intention. My intention is to help people understand Macmurray and Smith as a way to understand their own experience of God and their ministry. No matter how readers react to the book, my intention remains the same, and they continually encounter me whether they know it or not. The analogy to God's one action limps very badly, but nonetheless the analogy can give us a dim understanding of how we encounter God in this universe. The Kingdom of God, as noted earlier, can be understood as what God intends for the one action which is the universe. God, in other words, is working out God's intention of creating a universe where all human beings live in community with God, Father, Son, and Holy Spirit, and hence with one another. Whether we know it or not, whether we intend our actions to be in conformity with God's one action or not, in this universe we encounter God's intention and, in consequence, God at every moment of our existence because we are part and parcel of the universe which is God's one action.

Now this one action of God includes the incarnation of the Word of God, the second Person of the Trinity. Indeed, according to scripture and tradition our universe is created in view of the incarnation. Jesus of Nazareth, as the Epistle to the Colossians says, "is the image of the invisible God, the firstborn over all creation. . . . He is before all things, and in him all things hold together" (Col 1:15, 17). If anyone is the apple of God's eye, then surely it is Jesus. It would be strange indeed if Jesus never experienced the special love of the God he called "Abba." Perhaps the experience at the Jordan was precisely such an experience. But the experience does not require a special intervention of God for its explanation. God is always acting toward Jesus as "Abba." At this moment, we could say, Jesus' awareness of this fact was heightened.

Other Examples

In a similar way we can understand our own experiences of God. At times we will be in tune with God's one action, in harmony with God's will, and we may and probably do experience that harmony. We may, like the disciples on the road to Emmaus, feel our hearts burning within us, but not advert to the fact until later. After their eyes were opened at the breaking of the bread and Jesus disappeared, "(t)hey asked each other, 'Were not our hearts burning within us while he talked with us on the road and opened the Scriptures to us?' " (Lk 24:32). If we are praying imaginatively with the gospel text of Jesus' baptism, we may feel that God is delighted with us. As we savor that experience, we come to realize that we sense a new freedom, an openness to life, a oneness with God and God's hopes for the world. We may, for example, feel freed of the resentment at a friend who has wronged us. Could not this experience be an encounter with God's action in the world and thus with God? God does not intervene from outside the world to make the encounter possible. God is always immanent in the world because the world is God's one action, just as in an analogous way I am immanent in my action. And just as I am not my action, but transcend it in some real way, so too, and *a fortiori*, God is not his action, but transcends it.

God's One Creative Action Which Is the Universe

Let's look at the same idea from another viewpoint. In *Let This Mind Be In You*[24] Sebastian Moore leads one to the conclusion that we can experience our creation and thus experience in absolute fashion how desirable we are. God's desire for me makes me exist, indeed, makes me desirable. But God's creative act is never done; if it were, we would not exist. Hence, we should be able to experience our creation. Moore points to experiences of a welling up of desire for "I know not what." The desire is not for this or that lovely being although the occasion for the experience may be the presence of some lovely being. The desire is for the unnameable, the "All," the Mystery. This desire is the Joy by which C. S. Lewis was surprised.

Perhaps some examples from ordinary people collected by the Religious Experience Research Unit at Oxford University may help us to get a flavor of such an experience.[25]

> I heard nothing, yet it was as if I were *surrounded by golden light* and as if I only had to reach out my hand to touch God himself who was so surrounding me with his compassion.[26]

> It seemed to me that, in some way, I was extending into my surroundings and was becoming one with them. At the same time I felt a sense of lightness, exhilaration and power as if I was beginning to understand the true meaning of the whole universe.[27]

> One night I suddenly had an experience as if I was buoyed up by waves of utterly sustaining power and love. The only words that came near to describing it were "underneath are the everlasting arms," though this sounds like a picture, and my experience was not a

> picture but a feeling, and there were the arms. This I am sure has affected my life as it has made me know the love and sustaining power of God. *It came from outside and unasked.*[28]

> On the first night I knelt to say my prayers, which I had now made a constant practice, I was aware of a glowing light which seemed to envelop me and which was accompanied by a sense of warmth all round me.[29]

> Suddenly I felt a great joyousness sweeping over me. I use the word "sweeping" because this feeling seemed to do just that. I actually felt it as coming from my left and sweeping round and through me, completely engulfing me. I do not know how to describe it. It was not like a wind. But suddenly it was there, and I felt it move around and through me. Great joy was in it. Exaltation might be a better word.[30]

These examples could be experiences of being created as the apple of God's eye. They do not have to be understood as the experience of a "new" intervention into the world, but as the experience of God's one action which includes the creation of individuals. To return to Jesus' experience of his baptism: God loves Jesus in a special way as part of God's one action. That one action breaks through into the consciousness of Jesus in this scene. Moreover, the example brings out again the truth of John Smith's claim "that there is no experience of God that is not at the same time experience of something else."[31] By this he means that every experience of God is mediated. We might say that every experience of God is sacramental. Given the argument we have just concluded about the one action of God, we might add to Smith's statement: there is no experience of anything that is not at the same time an encounter with God. We may not and cannot always be aware that we are encountering God; hence, not every experience has a religious dimension for us. But in principle every human experience can have such a dimension because God is always present and active in the universe which is God's one action.

Experiences of God in Social Situations

At a recent international meeting Gerard Hughes, S.J., author of *The God of Surprises,* remarked that a number of people who have worked for peace and justice have experienced shame and confusion, a sense of their own complicity in the sinful social structures which they were trying to change. He remarked that such experiences are similar to the experiences of personal sinfulness when one is in the presence of the Holy One. I was reminded of experiences of immense sorrow and pain which others have shared with me as they contemplated the pain and suffering and injustice in the world. They and I have felt that we were experiencing God's attitude toward such evil. A married woman once told me of an ecstatic experience of God's presence right after intercourse with her husband. It was as if God were reveling in the couples' mutual love and letting her know of God's delight. I venture to say that these people were experiencing the desire of God for the primacy of love and of community between all people, rather than disunity and injustice.

The Role of the Spiritual Director

The arguments of Macmurray and Smith taken together give a rationale for the major role of the spiritual director, namely, to help directees pay attention to their experience as the locus of their encounter with God. Moreover, directors and directees need not confine themselves to discussions of formal prayer; on the basis of the present argument we can say that any experience can be examined to discover the mysterious Other whom we call God. Indeed, the more attentive one becomes to the presence of God in one's life, the more one becomes a contemplative in action, finding God quite literally in all things. Finally, this line of argument leads quite easily to an understanding of the necessity of discernment, both to discover what is of God in any experience, and to attune one's actions to the one action of God.

Near the end of his life Ignatius said that "each time and hour that he wanted to find God, he found Him."[32] Some might say that he attained this facility of finding God from infused contemplation. Perhaps they are right. I would, however, prefer to speculate that Ignatius gained this facility, with the aid of God's grace surely, by learning to notice differences, by becoming discerning. It is said that each day he engaged in frequent examens of consciousness, a practice which Aschenbrenner links to discernment.[33] I have come to believe that, for Ignatius, the examen in daily life functioned in much the same way as the reflection period suggested after each period of prayer in the *Spiritual Exercises.* After each period of prayer the retreatant is asked to spend a short period of time reflecting on what happened during the prayer. The purpose is to notice what happened and to discern what was of God from what was not. For Ignatius God not only creates all creatures, but also dwells in them and works in them.[34] Our own reflections have led us to affirm that every human experience can have a religious dimension, can be an encounter with God. On this assumption we meet God at every moment of the day, but we are not always aware of this reality. Thus, each period of the day can be considered a "period of prayer," a time when we meet God. The examen, then, becomes a period of reflection on a particular period of a day in order to become more aware of the touch of God. Fidelity to the examen helped Ignatius to become more and more fine-tuned to God's presence in his daily life. Thus, he could say that he could easily find God.

We might also note that the sessions of spiritual direction themselves are privileged times for reflection on our experience to discover in it the "rumor of angels."[35] But the sessions are also privileged times when both directee and director can experience God. The heightened awareness that talking about experiences of God produces in both director and directee makes the spiritual direction sessions themselves times to savor the religious dimension of existence. These sessions are "holy ground" indeed. The theological enterprise we are involved in supports the thrust of *The Practice of Spiritual Direction*. There we stressed the importance of paying attention to the experience of the directee. In workshops on spiritual direction I have only half facetiously said that directees should avoid directors who want to "help them." I would then explain that I looked for directors who were interested in God and in the experience of God because such directors would help people talk about such experience. If directors are not deeply interested in God, they might miss the experience of God that is going in the session itself in their haste to be "helpful."

The rules for the discernment of spirits in the book of the Exercises also are aimed to help people to discern in any experience or series of experiences what is of God from what is due to other influences. While Ignatius speaks of the influence of the evil spirit, we can speak of the influence of those other dimensions of human experience on the encounter with God. Fidelity to such discernment in daily life can gradually lead us to becoming contemplatives in action, i.e., people who walk and work and live more and more conscious of the presence of God, people who can tell the difference more and more easily between what is of God and what is not of God in any particular experience.

Conclusion

Reflection on human experience as an encounter between what there is and a being capable of encountering what there is and of reflecting on the encounter leads us to affirm the multidimensionality of any human experience. In order that an experience have a religious dimension two things are necessary, God who can be encountered directly and a person who is on the lookout for God. With Smith we have affirmed that the direct encounter with God is always mediated, i.e., that every encounter with God is an encounter with something else at the same time. For the believer God is both transcendent to this universe and immanent in it. Because of God's immanence God is always encounterable.[36] Human beings are not and cannot be always aware of God, but they can, with the help of God's grace, become more and more attuned to God's presence through fidelity to the kind of discernment entailed in the examen of consciousness. As we do so, we become more prompt to notice when "our hearts are burning within us" (Lk 24:32) as we walk the road of life. In this way we will come closer to that Ignatian ideal of finding God in all things, of being a contemplative in action.

4. *A Theology of Trinity and of Community*

Human beings, we have stated, encounter God in this world directly, but mediately. Thus far we have prescinded from the preeminent revelation of God in the New Testament, namely that the one God is a community of three whom tradition has named Father, Son or Word, and Holy Spirit. Two questions present themselves. Do we experience God as Trinity? How can we get a dim understanding of what this personal revelation of God means?

Karl Rahner makes the bald statement: "the Trinity of the economy of salvation *is* the immanent Trinity and vice-versa."[1] With this assertion he intends, I believe, what we have said earlier, namely that God is both transcendent to and immanent in this world and that the same God is both transcendent and immanent. If God is, apart from creation (i.e., what Rahner means by "the immanent Trinity"), three in One, then God is three in One as the Agent creating the world (i.e., in the economy of salvation). So if we encounter God in the world, we encounter God as Trinity.

The Experience of the Trinity

All well and good, and perfectly correct theologically. But do we in practice experience the Trinity? Rahner himself thought that most Christians were at best "modalists," i.e., people who quite unconsciously used the names Father, Son, Spirit indiscriminately for God as different modes of the one undifferentiated God.[2] We can only answer the question posed at the beginning of this paragraph by consulting our experience. If we have at one and the same time felt awed at the immensity of the universe and yet strangely safe, perhaps we have had the Father (or Mother) experience Jesus pointed to when he called God Abba, dear Dad. The experiences of our creation which I pointed to in the last chapter may be such experiences of God as Abba. As I put it in *God and You:*

> What is being described and hinted at here is an experience that has at least these elements: a sense of awe and mystery and a sense that one is safe with that mystery. The nearest analogy we have for such an experience is the experience of being held safely, snugly, and lovingly in a mother's or father's arms. Could this be one instance of the "Abba" experience, Mystery itself as "Dear Father" or "Dear Mother?"[3]

When people contemplate Jesus in the gospels, they often come to experience this very human Jewish male as someone supremely attractive and awesome. Moreover, they experience Jesus as having a very special relationship with the One he addressed as Abba, a relationship he wants to draw them into. Thus they find themselves reacting toward Jesus of Nazareth in the same way they react to the presence of Mystery Itself. In other words, they experience him as really human and contingent and yet feel the same way toward him as they feel toward God. In addition they experience Jesus as addressing God, even interceding for us before God. Such experiences led the early Christians to affirm that Jesus is Lord, and to be branded as blasphemers for doing so. Thus we do have experiences of Jesus as the Son of God in an absolutely unique way and affirm a distinction within the One God.

In *God and You* I asked how we experience the Holy Spirit and then raised these questions:

> Have you ever felt really depressed or terrified, yet found within yourself the strength to go on without

> knowing where the strength came from? Have you ever met someone who seemed to care profligately for you and for others and wondered where that love came from? Have you ever met really poor or suffering people and seen a light in their eyes that just did not seem to square with their situation? Have you ever experienced real care and love between people who should by all sociological and political accounts be at one another's throats? . . . Have you ever felt the power of the forces of hatred, greed, prejudice and violence in human hearts and wondered how they are held in check? Perhaps in any or all of these experiences we experience the light that the darkness cannot overcome, the Spirit or Life Breath of God that has been poured out into our hearts and the hearts of all men and women.[4]

A Theology of the Trinity

If we can, then, take it for granted that we do encounter God as Trinity in our world, we are left with the question of how to understand the experience, how to make some dim sense of this mystery that is the central self-revelation of God. Again Macmurray's philosophy can help us to a better understanding of the mysterious community which is the Trinity into which all human beings have been invited. In the first series of ten Gifford Lectures, published as *The Self as Agent,* Macmurray develops his philosophy of action and prescinds, for methodological reasons, from the interpersonal much as we prescinded from the Trinity in our discussion until now. The second series of lectures, *Persons in Relation,* makes up for that methodological precision.

In the second chapter we noted that Macmurray wants to understand what persons are on their own terms, not in terms of an analogy to the physical universe or to the biological. Through reflection on the person he concluded that the form or unity-pattern of the personal is a positive which includes and is constituted by its own negative. Action, for example, includes and is constituted by its negative, thought. When I am just thinking, I withdraw from action; thus thinking is the negative of action. But if I act, I know that I am acting and what I intend. Without knowledge there would be no action, only event. So, too, action includes and is constituted by its negative, event. No action takes place without including events, as we have seen in the second chapter. The form of the personal, therefore, is a positive which includes and is constituted by its own negative. In action I know myself and the Other (what is not I).

> We know existence by participating in existence. This participation is action. When we expend energy to realize an intention we meet a resistance which both supports and limits us, and know that we exist and that the Other exists, and that our existence depends upon the existence of the Other. Existence then is the primary datum. But this existence is not my own existence as an isolated self. If it were, then the existence of any Other would have to be proved, and it could not be proved. What is given is the existence of a world in which we participate—which sustains and in sustaining limits our wills.[5]

From this standpoint Macmurray argues conclusively that the unit of the personal is not the self-sufficient individual, but the "I and You." With this definition of the personal we have a conception that can be applied analogously to the Trinity.

Persons Are Constituted by Their Relations

"The idea of an isolated agent," says Macmurray, "is self-contradictory. Any agent is necessarily in relation to the Other. Apart from this essential relation he does not exist."[6] I cannot act except as part of the universe. But for human agents the Other must also be personal. "Persons are constituted by their mutual relation to one another. 'I' exist only as one element in the complex 'You and I'."[7] For present purposes I want to take this conclusion for granted. I also want to take for granted a further assertion, namely that this unit "You and I" is not just matter of fact, but matter of intention; "I" and "You" intend this relationship. Finally, let me underline a very important implication of these assertions. Without at least one "You" with whom "I" am in personal relation "I" do not exist as a person, since persons are constituted by their mutual relations. For believers God is, of course, the primordial "You" constituting any "I" because, if God did not desire the relationship, no "I" would exist.

With this understanding of what constitutes persons we have, I believe, a way of arriving at an analogous and dim understanding of how there can be three Persons in the one God. If persons are constituted by their relations, then we can agree with traditional Catholic trinitarian theology that the three Persons are constituted by their relations to one another.[8] In God what distinguishes the Persons from one another are their mutual relations and nothing else. Unlike human persons, however, the three Persons are not different beings, but one being, the Mystery we call God. Once again, we reflect on what constitutes human-beings persons, and use this most exalted characteristic of the human in an analogous fashion to get some dim understanding of the Mystery who is God. We are constituted persons by our mutual relations; so, too, the three Persons who are the one God are constituted by their mutual relations. What we deny in God is that the three Persons are different beings. From revelation we learn that persons do not have to be separate beings. Indeed, even here human persons may reveal that they are made in the "image and likeness" of God. Whenever two human persons are deeply in love, one of their most profound pains often arises from the fact that they cannot be absolutely one. Perhaps such pain indicates that we are pale images of the Trinity where the three Persons are only distinguished by their mutual relations and by nothing else. Perhaps, too, we can in this way give an explanation of why our hearts are restless until they rest in God, as Augustine so well said.

The Trinity as Community

The Trinity is the perfect community where nothing is lacking. These reflections should put paid to the romantic, but ultimately heretical, notion that God created the universe because he was lonely. Precisely because God is the perfect community, God had no need to create anything else. God creates the universe for no other motive than God's own gratuitous and unfathomable love. It is as if the three Persons said to one another: "Our community is so good; why don't we create a universe where we can invite others to share our community."

In this universe we encounter the Triune God who continually calls us into community. When we encounter the risen Jesus of Nazareth through contemplation of the gospels or even of another person, we encounter the One who from all eternity proceeds from the One whom Jesus called Abba. In a way which we cannot fathom the second Person of the Trinity, by the very fact of proceeding from the Father, can take on a human nature so completely that we can say of Jesus of Nazareth that he is the second Person of the Trinity and therefore God.[9] Because of this hypostatic union Jesus is the unique revelation of who God is. O'Donnell, following the German theologian Jüngel, says

> that the decisive moment where this revelation occurs is the death and resurrection of Jesus. In the paschal mystery, we see the event of revelation *par excellence*. God, who is beyond the world, identifies himself with this man Jesus, dead upon the cross. The implications of this identification are profound. First, we are challenged to think of God in union with the world. Secondly, we are led to think the eternal God in union with an historical event, in union with the temporal and perishable. Thirdly, we see here the union of life and death in such a way that God declares himself in favor of life rather than death. The paschal mystery is the triumph of life over the destructiveness of death.[10]

Notice that O'Donnell is, probably without intending it, demonstrating what Macmurray calls the form of the personal. The incarnation can only be understood as a positive (the second Person) who includes and is constituted by his negative (human nature). Without the human nature there would be no incarnation. Moreover, in the paschal mystery life (the positive) includes and is constituted by its negative (death). Without that concrete death on the cross this resurrected life would not be. Perhaps we get a dim understanding of Jesus' words about the necessity of the cross on the road to Emmaus: "Did not the Christ have to suffer these things and then enter his glory?" (Lk 24:26). Jesus of Nazareth in his very person and life reveals that God is self-emptying love, that God wants to include and be constituted by what is not God.

But we also believe that we are divinized (a favorite term of the Greek Fathers), brought into the community of the Trinity by the Holy Spirit who dwells in our hearts. Earlier in the chapter we pointed to experiences of the presence of the Holy Spirit. However, we are not hypostaticly united with the Spirit. O'Donnell notes that the Holy Spirit who proceeds from the Father and the Son (or from the Father through the Son)

> is always a relation of person to person. Whether in the Trinity, in the Incarnation or in the church, the Holy Spirit does not unite person to nature but person to person. Hence in the church the Spirit does not enter into a new hypostatic union. . . . In the church the Spirit unites the person of Christ to the person of each believer. At the same time the ground of unity among members of the Mystical Body is the same Spirit. Thus in the language of *Lumen Gentium* (no. 7), the Holy spirit is the soul animating the Mystical Body.[11]

O'Donnell argues for a personal indwelling of the Holy Spirit in each believer. Thus, in a mysterious fashion we participate in the community life of God by participating in the procession of the Holy Spirit from the Father and the Son. We participate in the relation of love which binds Father and Son together, the Spirit of God.

> The goal of God's trinitarian relations with the world is to make us partakers of the divine nature. Here is the recurring motif of the *admirabile commercium:* God has

become what we are, that we might become what he is. What Christ is by nature, we are by grace.[12]

The Community of the Church

Because the church is constituted by the indwelling of the Spirit in its members, O'Donnell argues, the church is not like an organization which people choose to join. We are chosen by Christ, and the source of our unity is "the person of the Holy Spirit dwelling both in Christ and in us."[13] Finally, because the Spirit does dwell in our hearts, the spiritual journey is "not only a restless striving toward God" but can also provide times of rest in the embrace of God.[14] But such "rest" can only come through surrender to the unique mission God has for each of us, which requires openness to the development of our relationship with God and discernment.

We can say, then, that we participate now in the community life of the Triune God. But we are painfully aware that we are sinners living in a sinful world. The community God intends seems more a pipe dream than a reality. We need to develop Macmurray's ideas on the form of the personal to gain a better understanding not only of what God intends but also of the obstacles and resistances we encounter and put up to God's intention.

The Problem of Community

We have already asserted, with Macmurray, that relationships are not matters of fact, but matters of intention; i.e., they are actions of the persons involved. Moreover, these actions which constitute relationships are motivated. Macmurray argues that our "distinguishable motives are relatively few and extraordinarily persistent."[15] He then shows that the original personal motivation has a positive and negative pole which he identifies as love and fear. These motives are personal motives because the behavior they motivate is communication and the need they express can only be answered by the action of another person. Love is for the other, the need to care for the other; fear is for the self, fear that the other will not respond to my need.

Macmurray uses the relationship of the infant and mother to illustrate this analysis of personal motivation. The human infant is totally dependent on a mothering person for everything, including life itself. Unless someone takes care of the infant, he or she will surely die. If that someone performs only the tasks needed for physical survival, but does not communicate caring, the infant will be stunted as a person and may even die. So the infant needs personal attention, needs to be loved (cared for) in order to develop as a person. But the infant is not just a passive recipient of caring. From the beginning the infant has at least two behaviors which communicate (even if the infant is not conscious of communicating): gurgles and coos of satisfaction and cries of dissatisfaction. The cries of dissatisfaction are motivated by discomfort and ultimately fear, the fear of pain, of hunger, of death at first and then, with growing recognition, the fear of loss of the caregiver. The gurgles and coos are motivated by satisfaction and rather quickly seem to become motivated by the presence of the caregiver; this latter motivation Macmurray calls love, a care for and delight in the other because the other is there for me. In the case of the infant we see the stark reality that underlies all intimate relationships: "Without you I am nothing or, at least, not the person I could be." This statement expresses the bipolar personal motivation of love and fear, love of your goodness and fear that you, who are so important to who I am, will withdraw your love. In the statement fear is subordinate to love and presupposes love.

Love and Fear

This bipolar motivation underlies all personal development from infancy on. Ideally fear is subordinated to love so that the prevailing motivation of the person is heterocentric, love for the other. However, even the best of parents are limited and sinful human beings, and so they will fail in some ways to fulfill the needs of their children in ways which enable the children to integrate and subordinate fear for the self under the prevailing motive of love for the other. Fear for oneself can become the predominant motive, and then the behavior that is motivated is predominantly defensive and egocentric. Moreover, all human relationships are problematic; even in those in which positive motivation dominates, unintegrated fear is also present and can break out in unintended behavior which is damaging to the relationship. How often it happens that we hurt close friends by questioning their motives or by jealousy, and we wonder where these surprising outbursts come from. All of us harbor fears for ourselves that are unintegrated into our positive motivation toward those whom we love.

Let us pause here to underline once again that the form of the personal shows itself here as well. Recall that the form of the personal is a positive which includes and is constituted by its negative. Here, love is the positive which includes and is constituted by its negative, fear. Love is for the other; fear is for the self. When fear predominates, I withdraw from love of the other into myself. In all human relationships some fear for oneself constitutes love for the other precisely because we all know that the loved other can fail us, can leave us, can die. In a fully realized personal relationship where love predominates, the other is the positive which includes and is constituted by its negative, the "I." Thus Macmurray can say, as we will presently see, that the ideal of the personal is a world where everyone cares for everyone else and no one cares for him/herself. The form of the personal requires charity as its ideal. In God, of course, we deny the existence of the negative, fear; each of the Persons "cares for" the Others and has no fear for the self. Once again, we conclude that we are pale images of God who nonetheless have the capacity to subordinate fear to love because of the Holy Spirit who dwells in our hearts.

Now if persons are constituted by their mutual relationships, any threat to an intimate relationship threatens the person's very being. Hence, the intensity of the emotions which accompany a significant change in a close relationship. It can feel like dying; one wonders how one can go on. A person may experience, with varying severity depending on the circumstances, all four of the stages of the dying process described by

Kübler-Ross: denial, anger, bargaining and depression, before finally coming to the fifth, acceptance (if one comes to it).[16] Indeed, the fear of death at its deepest level may be the fear of the loss of all meaningful relationships and thus of personal annihilation. Be that as it may, the human situation is the daunting one of needing significant others in order to be oneself. Moreover, what I need cannot be coerced; I cannot force you to love me. Even in the ordinary realm of personal relationships, therefore, we exist by grace and not by the strength of our own will. In fact, this is exactly how we receive real love, as gift, and our reaction is gratitude and joy, even if tinged by the fear that this cannot be happening to me.

Because of the vicissitudes of developmental history personal motivation may be predominantly heterocentric (other-centered) or predominantly egocentric. Heterocentric motivation means that love for the other dominates and subordinates fear for oneself. Such heterocentric motivation, if it is fully positive, must, however, be inclusive of all those with whom the person is in relation. If I am positively motivated toward you alone, then I must fear all others with whom we are related and, in the end, fear that you will join them and leave me. Fear will predominate over love. The argument can be repeated for groups of two, three, and so on. "We can therefore," says Macmurray, "formulate the inherent ideal of the personal. It is a universal community of persons in which each cares for all the others and no one cares for himself."[17] This ideal is, of course, realized only in the Trinity. It is the ideal of all universal religions and what Jesus seems to have meant by the Kingdom of God. In the first letter of John the ideal is expressed in this fashion: "There is no fear in love. But perfect love drives out fear, because fear has to do with punishment. The one who fears is not made perfect in love" (4:18). In the ideal no one has to care for self because that care is done by all the others. To the extent that I have to care for myself, to that extent fear is at work.

A predominantly egocentric motivation means that fear for oneself dominates and subordinates love for the other. Fear motivates defensive behavior, and one can defend oneself either by a submissive or by an aggressive attitude toward the other. In the first case I try to win from you by submission what I am afraid I cannot get from you freely. In the second I try to wrest from you by power what I want. Both kinds of behavior are self-defeating because what I really want and need is the mutuality of a personal relationship. Indeed, to the extent that fear predominates in my personal motivation, to that extent I am unfree. In a masterly paragraph Macmurray summarizes this part of his argument.

> I need you to be myself. This need is for a fully positive personal relation in which, because we trust one another, we can think and feel and act together. Only in such a relation can we really be ourselves. If we quarrel, each of us withdraws from the other into himself, and the trust is replaced by fear. We can no longer be ourselves in relation to one another. We are in conflict, and each of us loses his freedom and must act under constraint. There are two ways in which this situation can be met without actually breaking the relationship—which, we are assuming, is a necessary one. There may be a reconciliation which restores the original confidence; the negative motivation may be overcome and the positive relation reestablished. Or we may agree to co-operate on conditions which impose a restraint upon each of us, and which prevent the outbreak of active hostility. The negative motivation, the fear of the other, will remain, but will be suppressed. This will make possible co-operation for such ends as each of us has an interest in achieving. But we will remain isolated individuals, and the co-operation between us, though it may appear to satisfy our need of one another, will not really satisfy *us*. For what we really need is to care for one another, and we are only caring for ourselves. We have achieved society, but not community. We have become associates, but not friends.[18]

The three attitudes (heterocentric, submissive, or aggressive) lead to three different modes of apperception or typical ways of perceiving the world, especially the personal world. The heterocentric attitude leads a person to have positive expectations of others; the world of persons is expected to be a world where mutuality obtains. A predominantly egocentric attitude leads a person to negative expectations of others. The submissive attitude expects a world where conformity is demanded; the aggressive attitude expects a world where power talks.

Society versus Community

The next step of Macmurray's argument draws us close to the issue of how we live together. No matter what the prevailing mode of apperception and motivation, people need one another in order to exist and to flourish; hence, they must work out ways of living and working together. When one of these modes of apperception is dominant in a group, a particular form of society develops. If fear of the other is the predominant motivation, the members will have to work out ways of living and working together that protect against what is feared. Where the prevailing attitude is submissive, the society will develop ways of ensuring conformity without seeming to be coercive; "good form," "the way we do things" become the norms of behavior. Where the prevailing attitude is aggressive, the society will develop ways of ensuring the rights of all so that power does not get out of hand; law is the means and obedience to it becomes the norm of behavior.

Macmurray calls these two forms of association "societies," reserving the word community for the association of persons where the prevailing motivation is heterocentric and the prevailing mode of apperception is what he calls communal. Once again I must cite Macmurray at length (italics mine).

> Any community of persons, as distinct from a mere society, is a group of individuals united in a common life, the motivation of which is positive. Like a society, a community is a group which acts together; but unlike a mere society its members are in communion with one another; they constitute a fellowship. A society whose members act together without forming a

> fellowship can only be constituted by a common purpose. They cooperate to achieve a purpose which each of them, in his own interest, desires to achieve, and which can only be achieved by co-operation. The relations of its members are functional; each plays his allotted part in the achievement of the common end. The society then has an organic form: it is an organization of functions; and each member is a function of the group. A community, however, is a unity of persons as persons. *It cannot be defined in functional terms, by relation to a common purpose.* It is not organic in structure, and cannot be constituted or maintained by organization, but only by the motives which sustain the personal relations of its members. *It is constituted and maintained by a mutual affection.* This can only mean that each member of the group is in positive personal relation to each of the others taken severally. The structure of a community is the nexus or network of the active relations of friendship between all possible pairs of its members.[19]

Community means friendship; its primary bond is the mutual love of its members, not some ulterior purpose. But we must say more. Such community is what all human beings long for; we want to live without fear, or at least with our fears integrated and subordinated to our love. In the universe God is creating this desire wells up in us because it is what God wants. We want to live in mutual fellowship, but we cannot do it on our own; that is *the* human problematic, a problematic religion alone can resolve. Christianity, for one, offers a solution: belief in a God who is the perfect community, who invites each of us into that community, and whose Spirit dwelling in our hearts enables us to cast out our fears and love one another. Because God wants and enables community, it can and does exist; the human desire for community is not chimerical because God is love. Wherever real religion exists, the thrust toward community in Macmurray's sense also exists. Indeed, real religion is the celebration of communion, a celebration of the community which exists and a pointer and incentive toward the community yet to be.

Christian Community

If the argument thus far is valid, then we must conclude that any grouping of people in direct relationship that is really Christian is at least inchoatively a group of friends, or people who love one another in the Lord. The primary motivation for their togetherness is their friendship in the Lord and their desire to celebrate that friendship. The primary purpose is not to feed the hungry, to educate their children, to take care of the sick, but to enjoy one another's company in celebration of the Lord. Of course, because they love one another and that love is outgoing, they may together decide to do any or all of these other things. Indeed, such "works" demonstrate their love or flow from their love, but they do not constitute them a community (just as, analogously, our universe flows from the love of the Trinity but does not constitute the community of the Trinity). Again we see that we are a pale image of the Triune God. Christians in direct relationship are a community because they love one another. This conclusion applies to a couple, a family, a parish, a prayer group, a group of Jesuits, of Ursulines, of Benedictines, or of Opus Dei. Of course, there will be a gradation of friendship in the group, but the "glue" that makes them a community is their mutual care for one another in the Lord. And that "glue" is produced by the indwelling Spirit of God. The examples chosen also indicate that community as Macmurray understands it does not require that the members live together, only that they be in direct relationship and intend mutual friendship in the Lord.

Hence, a community of religious people is constituted by the intention of the members to be and become friends in the Lord, to let God overcome their fears of one another so that mutual love prevails. But any community of believers is problematic. Since it depends on the intention of its members, all of whom are sinners with unintegrated fears, the intention may be withdrawn and fear may prevail. Community, like marriage and any friendship, requires attention and work. There must be opportunities for celebration and for sharing and for reconciliation, especially opportunities for celebrating and sharing their mutual love of the Lord who brings them together. Any community is an endangered species and, therefore, needs tending.

> The continuous possibility that hostility and enmity may break out between members of the community and destroy the fellowship is inseparable from any consciousness of it. For community is a matter of intention and therefore problematical. . . . Moreover, the community so far achieved is imperfect, and contains not merely the possibility but also the evidences of failure.[20]

The opportunities for celebration, sharing, and reconciliation strengthen the motivation of love and help exorcise fears and overcome resentments.[21]

An Objection

Often enough an objection forms at about this point of the argument. Focus on community seems self-serving and narcissistic. Christian community is not for its own sake, but for the sake of the world. Macmurray would not disagree with the last statement. Indeed, in the Swarthmore Lectures he says quite bluntly: "Christianity is not for the sake of the Christians, but *for the sake of the world,*" and goes on to define the church as "the community of the disciples of Jesus working, in co-operation with God and under the guidance of His Spirit, to establish the Kingdom of Heaven on earth."[22] Apparently he does not believe that the notion of community as a grouping of people who love one another is incompatible with service of the world. The objection, I believe, arises from the application of the concept of energy to personal relations.

I am more and more convinced that the energy analogy is dangerous when used to explain aspects of the spiritual life or even of any interpersonal life that is not neurotic. Energy in physics is a finite quality; if a certain amount is expended in one direction, then that amount is unavailable for something else.

Thus, the objection to focus on community life is that such a focus absorbs energy that might better be used for the apostolate. What we forget is that the energy analogy when applied in psychology attempts to explain human action as determined, hence unfree. In fact, energy explanations only work for neurotic behavior, behavior that is determined by the past. In experience, real love for anyone cannot be explained by energy dynamics; real love by its nature seems inexhaustible, tending toward the inclusion of more and more people.

In *Let This Mind Be In You*[23] Sebastian Moore points out that the prophets do not argue from the human analogy to qualities of God, but the other way around. Hosea, for example, would not have it in his heart to forgive his harlot wife if he and Israel had not already experienced God as forgiving their harlotry. Jesus does not argue from the way one human being forgives another to the way God forgives. Rather, we are asked to be perfect as our heavenly Father is perfect. Moore's insight suggests to me the model of the Trinity as the best way to understand the ideal of human community. The three Persons in God are perfectly happy with one another; they are the perfect community where nothing but their mutual relations to one another distinguish them. Yet they freely decide to include in their interpersonal life a universe of creatures. Obviously, their love is not governed by energy dynamics. But that love is poured out into our hearts. So if that love subordinates our fears and enables community to be, it is of its nature inclusive, not exclusive. Where real community exists, we should expect to see it as outgoing, rather than narcissistic.

Thus, the problem is not that the existence of a community of friends in the Lord will take away energy from Christian praxis. Rather, the problem is that a grouping of Christians that is not sufficiently a community does operate on energy dynamics and is exhausting because fear of one another rather than love prevails. Then the group's interactions are governed by convention or by law, or by both. A group governed by convention resembles the caricature of the English men's club where "good form" is the norm of behavior. A group governed by law resembles what many religious "communities" have been. In one sense both "good form" and law do free up energy for work. They control the fear of one another and enable smooth functioning so that the individuals can do their work. But what is the purpose of that work? If it is apostolic, then the work must somehow be in tune with the ministry of Jesus and the intention of God. That intention, however, is best expressed in the double commandment of love of God and love of neighbor. If the individuals in a "community" fear one another more than they love one another, are they not in the position of the blind leading the blind in their "apostolic" work?

Thus, I argue that groups of Christians must intend to be communities, first of all, because that is what the Lord wants of any grouping of his followers, secondly because that alone will satisfy their members' deepest desires, and thirdly because only such communities preach by their very being that God is the perfect community of love. And I argue that the real effectiveness of a group's apostolate varies directly with the group's approximation to being friends in the Lord. Finally, I venture to say that religious groups will attract followers in direct proportion to their approximation to being friends in the Lord.

The most insidious voice that hinders us from even desiring community of the sort envisaged is that voice of reason in us that says: "You can't expect that ideal in practice; be realistic. Christian community isn't a family, and it's foolish to expect it to be." This "voice of reason" has strong persuasive powers, but it must be seen for what it really is, the voice of fear, indeed, the voice of sin. If we give credence to this voice, we will stifle those Spirit-inspired desires and hopes for something better, for a community of friends in the Lord.

While we must not let the voice of sin drown out the whispers of hope, we need to recognize with Macmurray that personal relationships are problematic because in all of us there is unintegrated fear. Thus, in all of us who hope to be part of a community of friends there is the possibility of the dominance of egocentric motivation and defensive behavior. Indeed, an honest look at most of what passes for Christian "community" would force us to admit that, in Macmurray's terms, they are societies, not communities, where "good form" or law rule behavior. We need to bend every effort to create the conditions that make real community possible.

Conclusion

In this chapter we have argued that our encounter with God is an encounter with the perfect community of Father, Son and Holy Spirit whose intention in creating the universe is to invite human beings to become part of their community, and thus to live in harmony with one another and with the whole of creation. Fear gets in the way of our accepting the invitation and thus is the root of all evil in the world. We cannot attain the deepest desire of our hearts, union with the Triune God, apart from human community, and that human community has to be universally inclusive at least in intention. So the church is absolutely necessary for our salvation. But, unfortunately, because of unintegrated fears in all their members every real church is only a pale image of the ideal church, the Kingdom of God. Still the churches, for all their imperfections, do keep alive the message of Jesus and thus do keep before all of us the dream of God.[24]

5. The Development of the Relationship with God

If fear is the root of all evil in the world, religion's role is the overcoming of fear. But the overcoming of fear cannot be illusory. Religion must not become the opium of the people. In a remarkable aphorism Macmurray contrasts illusory religion with real religion:

> The maxim of illusory religion runs: "Fear not; trust in God and He will see that none of the things you fear will happen to you"; that of real religion, on the contrary, is "Fear not; the things that you are afraid of are quite likely to happen to you, but they are nothing to be afraid of."[1]

How can a person come to real religion, which means a belief in the real God of Mystery and love, the God who is Father, Son and Holy Spirit, the God who has stooped to conquer all that we fear by taking on what is not God?

The Necessity of Other People

First of all, obviously, a person must meet someone or some people who themselves have encountered and believe in the God of Jesus Christ. St. Paul puts it thus:

> How, then, can they call on the one they have not believed in? And how can they believe in the one of

> whom they have not heard? And how can they hear without someone preaching to them? And how can they preach unless they are sent? As it is written, "How beautiful are the feet of those who bring good news!" (Rom 10:14–15)

The ceremony of light at the Easter Vigil liturgy has a wonderful symbol of evangelization. When the Easter candle is lit from the new fire, it symbolizes the risen Christ. Then gradually the candles of all those in the church are lit from the one candle, but not directly. In the darkness each person receives the light from the person nearest him/her and the light is passed on. In the darkness of the church the face of each person emerges from the shadow as he/she receives the light from the person nearest. But the source of all the light is the Easter candle which symbolizes the risen Christ. So the first thing to be said about how we come to a belief in the real God is that it comes through others, through a community of people who have believed in the Father of the Lord Jesus Christ, i.e., through the church.

For most people the family is the first community through which the light is passed on. Some sense of the universe as a place of basic trust is communicated to most infants by the care and love they receive that keeps them alive. But, as we have already noted, even the best of parents have their own unintegrated fears and hostilities which cannot help but infect in some way their children. So all of us grow up with unintegrated fear. Erikson's "basic trust"[2] is at best a more or less quality in us, not an absolutely solid foundation upon which we move ahead into life and into our relationship with God. It may be well for us to spend some time discussing the development of this relationship with God and others in the light of the theology we have been pursuing.

A Developmental Pattern

Persons are defined by their relations, as we have noted, and the ideal of religion is an inclusive community in which everyone cares for everyone else and no one cares for him/herself. In other words, what God wants for us is that we become, in Macmurray's terms, heterocentric in our motivation toward others. But this ideal is endangered by our unintegrated fears, fears which can evolve into hatreds. With these assumptions we can describe the developmental pattern of any relationship, including the relationship with God, on a continuum running from a cold, emotionally distant, highly stylized relationship between a person and others and God to the mystical union of a person with God and the ideal of community described earlier.

Since the developmental pattern is conceived as a continuum, a person can be anywhere along the line. I will try to sketch out a developmental pattern that corresponds to an interpersonal view of the dynamic of the *Spiritual Exercises*.[3] In this description I am talking about the experience someone has of God or another person, not about God's actual attitude and relationship to the person nor about the other person's actual attitude. A person's experience of another can be largely a projection of his/her own fears and past relationships.

The Affective Principle and Foundation

A person at the very low end of the continuum experiences God and others as very distant, cold, demanding and frightening. The first real step toward a closer relationship comes with the experience that the other person really cares for me which elicits from me the response of gratitude to and trust in that person. When this attitude is relatively firmly established in me, I have what might be called the affective foundation for the positive development of the relationship. In the case of the relationship with God what needs to be established is what I have called the affective Principle and Foundation.[4] The British psychiatrist J. S. Mackenzie states quite well what I mean.

> The *enjoyment of God* should be the supreme end of spiritual technique; and it is in that enjoyment of God that we feel not only saved in the Evangelical sense, but safe: we are conscious of belonging to God, and hence are never alone; and, to the degree we have these two,

> hostile feelings disappear. . . . In that relationship Nature seems friendly and homely; even its vast spaces instead of eliciting a sense of terror speak of the infinite love; and the nearer beauty becomes the garment with which the Almighty clothes Himself.[5]

Henry Guntrip, who cites Mackenzie, himself notes: "It is a common experience in psychotherapy to find patients who fear and hate God, a God who, in the words of J. S. Mackenzie 'is always snooping around after sinners'. . ." Many Christians seem to have such an attitude toward God. What such people need is help to experience God as different from the God they fear. Those who minister in the church need to develop the spiritual techniques or pastoral practices that will help people to come to a basic trust in God, to have, and to have confidence in, these foundational experiences.

This affective principle and foundation can be called the experience of having a spiritual identity, a real relationship to God. It is the experience of wholeness that allows one to know brokenness, the experience of being loved and lovely that precedes the experience of sinfulness, the experience of enjoyment and oneness with God that enables a person to see the present state of self and world as a fall from grace. Without such an experience of God's primordial love and care a person remains rooted in a distant, perhaps scrupulous, perhaps resentful relationship with God.

To establish this foundation firmly may take a long time. Blessed Peter Faber, one of the first companions of St. Ignatius, lived in the same student rooms with Ignatius and Francis Xavier. For four years Ignatius would not give him the full spiritual exercises because, by his own admission, Faber was full of scruples and had a terrible fear of God.[6] Ignatius gave him what we would now call much pastoral care and counseling to help him to have a foundational experience of God. Resistance to a closer relationship with God prior to the foundational experience derives primarily from the false images of God people have formed during their early years. Hence, the work of the spiritual director or minister at this stage is to help people to experience God in a more benign way.

The Rhythm of Withdrawal and Return

After developing his ideas on how the basic motivations of fear and love develop in the child, Macmurray then shows that the pattern of personal development in the child is one of a rhythm of withdrawal and return. When the child's motivation is basically controlled by love, then she and the other are in harmony and friendship (provided, of course, that the other is also motivated by love). Fear for herself is subordinated to love for the other. But, as we have already indicated, in every one there are unintegrated fears which can break out and gain the upper hand. When this happens in the child, she withdraws from the positive relationship out of fear for herself. For the positive relationship to be restored there must be some sort of reconciliation. In the child, at least, the reconciliation depends on the attitude taken by the other. If the other continues to act out of love, then the child's fear for herself can be overcome and the relationship of communion can be reestablished. This pattern of withdrawal and return also characterizes all our relationships throughout our lives, including our relationship with God. The withdrawal shows itself in our resistance to God's offers of intimacy, and the return in the overcoming of the resistance. The latter always requires the grace of God. In what follows we shall see how this pattern of withdrawal and return continually characterizes the development of our relationship with God as well as with one another.[7]

Withdrawal Because of Real Sin

Once the foundation is firmly established, the next step seems to be taken when people experience themselves as sinners. The human analogy is the end of the "honeymoon" period in a relationship when the two people have a falling out and begin to wonder about one another's continued love, given the falling out and the hurt each has received and given. Unintegrated fears can take over and each person is dominated by fear for the self rather than by love for the other. Toward God something similar occurs. While the foundational experience of God's love comes as a surprise and feels undeserved, at this new stage people begin to see themselves as unworthy because of personal sin. "God created me out of love and brought me into his friendship. Look what I have done to him! Could God really still love me with all my past sins and my present sinfulness?" God seems distant once more.

In her spiritual mystery novel *Glittering Images* Susan Howatch gives a graphic example of this state of sin and delusion. The Anglican priest Charles Ashworth has sinned grievously and almost in despair has come to the Abbot of the Fordite monastery in a drunken state for spiritual help. He wakes up with a hangover and the abbot walks into his room. The following dialogue takes place.

> I gasped: "I'm cut off from God." I was in terror. I was shuddering from head to foot. Tears were streaming down my face. "He's gone. He's rejected me. He's not here—"
> "He's here but you can't see Him. You've been blinded."
> "Blinded—"
> "It's only temporary but meanwhile you must do exactly as I say. Let's try to get you up from the floor—and onto the bed—that's it—"
> "I'm being invaded." I was shuddering again, gasping for breath. "Without God—all the demons—taking over—telling me I'm not fit to—"
> "Take this." He shoved his pectoral cross hard into my hand. "The cross bars their path. No demon can withstand the power of Christ."
> *"But he's not here—"*
> "He's here. He's here whenever his followers are gathered together in his name. He's here."[8]

The withdrawal from and resistance to closeness to God now seem to come from the realization of how "unholy" one is before the Holy One. The resistance here, too, is based on an illusion, but one founded on the fact of one's sinfulness. The illusion, however, is the belief that God does not love sinners, especially when they are stuck in sin. God comes close again (in experience) when I realize that God so loved me, sins and all, that he let his beloved Jesus die for me. I personally accept Jesus' dying for me even though Jesus and the Father know exactly who I have been and am. This experience also takes time and may need to be repeated in many different ways, but when it takes root, it frees people radically and relatively permanently from the kinds of crippling fears that keep them focused primarily on themselves and their own protection. The response is gratitude and the desire to do something for the Lord. At least by this stage of the journey there is an experience of a distinction of persons in God since Jesus and God are experienced as somehow distinct, yet identical.

At this stage also people may experience the pervasiveness of sin and sinful structures in our world and in themselves. If personal sinfulness can seem so intractable, rendering us almost despairing of a conversion of heart, how much more powerless we feel before the enormous social, political and economic problems we face today! It sometimes seems better not to read the newspaper nor to watch the news on television. Darkness does threaten to overcome the light. Consumerism, racism, nationalistic prejudices, the arms race—these cultural and social forces seem to rule us and our world. In our present world and church, the experience of being freed from the tyranny of sin[9] needs to include a relative freedom from the overpowering sense of being trapped by these dark forces. With St. John we need to come to the felt conclusion that the light has not been and will never be overcome by the darkness (Jn 1:5), that, in fact, our fears are illusory.[10]

The Following of Jesus

This experience of radical freedom from the fear that oneself and our world have been rejected by God shifts a person's focus away from the self and toward the Other. Of course, fear does not entirely disappear, but it becomes more integrated under the more powerful dynamism of love. People who are ready and willing are led into the dynamic of a developing relationship with Jesus. They want to know Jesus better, to know his values, his dreams, his vision, his loves and hates, in order to love him more and follow him more closely. The dynamism for this desire is the Holy Spirit who draws each of us toward a more intimate relationship with Jesus. As they progress in this dynamic of companionship, they experience the attraction of Jesus, but also the resistance to and fear of being chosen as his companions. Again we see the rhythm of withdrawal due to fear, but here the resistance to a deeper intimacy with Jesus is much more realistic; those who take on the values of Jesus do often suffer persecution and martyrdom. But once again, we recall Macmurray's maxim of real, as distinct from illusory, religion: ". . . the things you are afraid of are quite likely to happen to you, but they are nothing to be afraid of." If fears of loss and suffering dominate our hearts, then we cannot have what we most deeply want at this stage, namely intimate friendship with Jesus. With the help of God's grace people are enabled to beg to be chosen as companions and to be imbued with the spirit of Jesus. They want to be affectively and effectively united with Jesus where affective union means being united with Jesus' goals and strategies.

We notice here that the focus is on Jesus and on working together with him and others of like mind. The human analogy is the couple who are sufficiently anchored in their mutual love that they can become generative, or the community sufficiently sure of its own cohesiveness that it can reach out to include others in its care and concern. Intimacy with Jesus leads to the desire to be of service to others and to confront unjust powers and structures just as Jesus did. Intimacy with Jesus, if it is real, does not lead to a treacly "me and Jesus" spirituality feared by some social activists.

Participating in the Suffering, Death and Resurrection of Jesus

The clearest indication that one person cares for the other and not so much for the self is the willingness to share the other's sufferings and dying. Suffering and dying people often feel a terrible loneliness because their loved ones cannot bear to be with them in any real way, cannot bear to be present to their sufferings and agony. It is a sign of great unselfishness that a friend wants to share the agony of a dying friend. So, too, it is a sign of great development in the relationship with Jesus when a person really desires to share Christ's sufferings, to be privy to his inner state in the passion, and finally to share his experience of glory. Those who have moved this far along the continuum will be converted to the full reality of this world and be well on the way to finding God in all things quite literally.[11] Moreover, they will discover that the love poured out by the Spirit into their hearts has subordinated most of their fears under itself. With the risen Christ they live, as Sebastian Moore puts it, no longer "under the shadow of death," but "in the light with death behind" them. "The virus of eternity has entered" their "bloodstream forever."[12] By grace they participate in the joy of the resurrection now.

The Continued Possibility of Regression

Even though the development is pictured as on a linear continuum, experience teaches that the stages are not fixed positions from which there is no regression. A very deep experience of the Lord's forgiving love, for example, may not and usually does not touch every aspect of the person. Later in life a new dimension of sinfulness may be uncovered which can call into question all of the growth in relationship that has gone on. New life crises can also shatter a sense of security and bring on old fears of God. Such "regressions" happen frequently to all of us. But if the original conversion formed a solid base, the person will, with relative ease, be able to return to the earlier level of relationship. Moreover, I have noticed that some people who have suffered traumas in childhood only recall them when they contemplate in some depth the sufferings of Jesus. Such experiences catapult them once again into the need of personal healing, but they are accompanied by a sense that somehow or other the crucifixion of Jesus still goes on in the suffering of the innocent. Such an experience helps them to grasp how deeply God has become one with suffering humanity. I believe that such experiences are instances of the form of the personal. God not only embraces what is not God, but he even embraces the twisted, evil forces that impel human beings to abuse and torture the innocent. There is nothing more opposite God than such evil.

The Deepest Source of Withdrawal

Before I close this chapter I want to touch upon another source of resistance to closeness which seems even more at the heart of the matter than those sources we have touched upon thus far. We have noted sources of resistance that reside in our false images of God or in the real consequences of following Jesus. Deeper than any of these sources of resistance, I believe, is the fear of God's very being.[13] When we get close to God, we feel heartened, whole, joyful and grateful. Yet often enough, we find that right after such positive experiences of God we neglect prayer and have little time for God. When we "know" God (in the Johannine sense of "know-love"), we know in our depths that we are just our little selves, just John, Mary, Joan, with a very limited time on earth, with a very limited role to play in the history of the world and in salvation history. The positive reactions come from the realization that, in spite of our limitations, our sinfulness, our smallness, God, Mystery itself, still loves us and desires us as the "apple of God's eye." But what we also have to accept is the reality that we are just who we are, not God, nor even great players in the drama of the universe. Gerald May notes:

> Spiritual experience becomes even more threatening if it is viewed as an accurate perception of the way-things-are rather than some kind of isolated "high." Specifically, when one is in the midst of such experience, one cannot be in the business of defining oneself. . . . One's ego, sense of identity, self-image seem to evaporate almost magically. And one is left, just simply being.[14]

Conclusion

The paradoxical truth is that we can only have ourselves if we acknowledge the truth of ourselves, can only be ourselves if we surrender ourselves to the Mystery we call God. This is the paradoxical truth spoken by Jesus in John's gospel.

> The hour has come for the Son of Man to be glorified. I tell you the truth, unless a kernel of wheat falls to the ground and dies, it remains only a single seed. But if it dies, it produces many seeds. The man who loves his life will lose it, while the man who hates his life in this world will keep it for eternal life. Whoever serves me must follow me; and where I am, my servant will also be. My Father will honor the one who serves me.
>
> Now my heart is troubled, and what shall I say? "Father, save me from this hour?" No, it was for this very reason I came to this hour. Father, glorify your name.
>
> Then a voice came from heaven, "I have glorified it, and will glorify it again" (Jn 12:23–28).

Once again we come to the realization that we human beings have a very limited role to play in the unfolding of the one action of God which is the universe, namely to accept the call to communion with the Trinity and with one another without earning our way. This is a hard saying indeed for our egos. Yet it is really for our peace.

6. A Theology of Discernment of Spirits

We have argued that God's intention for the one action which is the universe is that it be the environment for a community of all persons (including the angels or "powers" of the scriptures and of tradition) with the Trinity. However, human life and community in this world is problematic, as we have repeatedly said. Community with one another is bedevilled by fear, as is community with God. If "I" am constituted a person by my relationships, the fear of losing relationships comes down to the fear of annihilation of myself. So at the root of all our fears is the fear of death, of annihilation.[1] Whatever the source, fear keeps us in either subservient or antagonistic relations with one another. If we do form bonds of community with some people, the fear shows itself in our attempts to make the community exclusive, "us and not them." Only perfect love casts out fear, as the First Letter of John says, and our peace lies in attaining that perfect love, or at least moving toward it. That perfect love is the will of God. Hence, the ultimate happiness of each individual resides in trying to align him- or herself with this will of God. Moreover, since perfect love cannot be attained until all human beings are one community, what is for my peace must also be for the peace of all humanity or lead toward it. In the ideal order, then, my desire as a Christian is to have all my actions in tune with the one action of God which intends a world community of perfect love.

Based on our analysis thus far fear is the culprit that keeps us out of tune because fear motivates defensive thinking and action. When I am more dominated by fear than by love, for example, my attitude toward the world and toward others is egocentric. I tend to see myself as alone in this world and required to protect myself by my own wits. In the final analysis, if my heart is governed by fear for myself, I am led to the illusion that no one loves me and that my only salvation can come from perpetual vigilance; in other words, I am my own savior. The paradox is that the more I am governed by fear for myself and, therefore, the more helpless and vulnerable I feel, the more I think that I must—and can—control my own destiny. An example may illustrate the paradox. As we were ending some years of spiritual direction because of a new assignment I had to undertake, a directee, for a few moments, felt very afraid and vulnerable. The thought flashed through his mind, "If I had prayed better, Bill would not be leaving me." When he told me about it, we both could smile at the recognition that this thought was putting all the control of my life in his hands. Unintegrated fear leads to illusory thinking and to intentions that frustrate our actions.

The Modern Crisis

Macmurray came to see that the crisis of the western world could be traced to the underdevelopment of humanity's affective side. He argued cogently in a series of talks on the BBC in 1930 and 1932 that westerners had successfully passed through one crisis at the time of the breakup of the medieval world by allowing the mind to develop in freedom. Modern science and technology and modern methods of historical and literary criticism are the result of the success of this revolution. The successful conclusion of this crisis had not been easy, but westerners had chosen "to trust one another to think for ourselves and to stand by the expression of our honest thought."[2] This choice had led to the great expansion of knowledge and technology that has so changed the world we know from anything past. Macmurray believed, however, that the affective life of westerners, at least of western men, had not developed concomitantly.

> As a result we are intellectually civilized and emotionally primitive; and we have reached the point at which

> the development of knowledge threatens to destroy us. Knowledge is power, but emotion is the master of our values and of the uses, therefore, to which we put our power. Emotionally we are primitive, childish, undeveloped. Therefore, we have the tastes, the appetites, the interests and apprehensions of children. But we have in our hands a vast set of powers, which are the products of our intellectual development. We have used these powers to construct an intricate machinery of life, all in the service of our childish desires. And now we are waking up to the fact that we cannot control it; that we do not even know what we want to do with it. So we are beginning to be afraid of the work of our hands. That is the modern dilemma.[3]

In the years following these words our world has seen those triumphs of unbridled intellect such as the ovens of Auschwitz, the atomic bombs dropped on Hiroshima and Nagasaki, the Gulag Archipelago, and state-sponsored terror in Argentina, Chile, Guatemala, El Salvador and elsewhere.

Macmurray asserted that the only way out of this modern dilemma was through the disciplined development of our affective lives. He believed that our feelings could become attuned to reality and in this sense become rational. But there is no "cheap grace."

> We shall have to submit to the discipline of our feelings, not by authority nor by tradition, but by life itself. It will not guarantee us security or pleasure or happiness or comfort; but it will give us what is more worth having, a slow, gradual realization of the goodness of the world and of living in it.[4]

And Macmurray believed, contrary to the tradition of the western world, that feeling is more important than thought. "It is in the hands of feeling, not of thought, that the government of life should rest. And in this I have the teaching of the founder of Christianity on my side, for he wished to make love—an emotion, not an idea—the basis of the good life."[5] Moreover, he argued that feeling is not blind nor chaotic, but "has its own principle of order in itself, and will control and guide itself if it is given the chance."[6]

C. S. Lewis makes a similar point, I believe, when he speaks of Joy as the desire for "I know not what." Lewis describes the experience of this Joy as "one of intense longing" which is distinguished from other longings by two things. First, the longing, though intense and even painful, is somehow a delight. Second, we can easily be mistaken about the object of the desire. In fact, for most of his life until his conversion to Christianity Lewis tried to satisfy this desire with objects that did not satisfy and could not satisfy the desire. He concludes:

> It appeared to me therefore that if a man diligently followed this desire, pursuing the false objects until their falsity appeared and then resolutely abandoning them, he must come out at last into the clear knowledge that the human soul was made to enjoy some object that is never fully given—nay, cannot even be imagined as given—in our present mode of subjective and spatio-temporal experience.[7]

Both Macmurray and Lewis felt that there is an inner logic in our affections that leads to the heart of reality and that can be discovered through a disciplined attention to our experience.

The reality of the world we inhabit is that it is continually being created by God to draw all persons and things into union with the community life of God. Those who do not believe in this reality are irrational in that their minds are not attuned with reality. Moreover, those who do not, at least, try to attune their own actions with God's one action are acting irrationally. But what motivates action is our affective life, and here once again we return to Macmurray's BBC lecture. Feeling is that in us which,

> when it is real feeling, . . . enables us to grasp the worth of things. Good and evil, beauty and ugliness,

> significance and value of all kinds are apprehended by feeling, not by thought. Without feeling we could know neither satisfaction nor dissatisfaction; nothing would be more worth while to us than anything else. In that case we could not choose to do one thing rather than another; and we could not even think, because we could not choose anything to think about, nor feel that one thought was more significant than another.[8]

Of course, we must also correctly assess the conditions of the world and thus use our minds.[9] It is feeling, however, which motivates us to act at all. Moreover, feeling which is in tune with the Holy Spirit who is the Spirit of love in this world will motivate action that intends what God intends, a real community of love between all people. If we can get our fears subordinated to love, then we can more easily attune our intentions with the one intention of God in creating this universe.

The Discernment of Spirits

The Experience of Being Out of Tune

With this argument we come to the theme of discernment of spirits. In his "Rules for Discerning the Spirits" in the *Spiritual Exercises* Ignatius proposes a method by which we can attune our motives and feelings with the one action of God. In the very first rules for the discernment of spirits he outlines the functions of the differing spirits that move us depending on the general direction of our lives. To the extent that I am out of tune with the one action of God, to that extent I will experience myself as alienated, unhappy, unfulfilled. I may not know the reason for my malaise and blame it on failed opportunities, the stupidity or bad will of others, or an upset stomach. I may look for all sorts of anodynes to relieve the malaise. I may seek relief in work, in relationships, in commitment to a great cause, in alcohol, in drugs. But none of these satisfy me because what I really desire is to live in community without fear. These feelings of malaise are, I believe, what Ignatius calls the actions of the "good spirit" in his first rule for the discernment of spirits.

> In the case of those who go from one mortal sin to another, the enemy is ordinarily accustomed to propose apparent pleasures. He fills their imagination with sensual delights and gratifications, the more readily to keep them in their vices and increase the number of their sins.
>
> With such persons the good spirit uses a method which is the reverse of the above. Making use of the light of reason, he will rouse the sting of conscience and fill them with remorse.[10]

In other words, when I am out of tune with the one action of God, when I am acting predominantly out of fear for myself rather than out of love for others, then I experience the action of God as a rasping of my spirit, as it were, as a sting of conscience in my good moments, a sting I try to anesthetize as much as possible in my bad moments. God continually acts in the universe to draw all of us into community with the Trinity and with one another. When we act counter to that action, we experience ourselves as somehow at sixes and sevens with ourselves and with others. In this theory there is no need of special interventions by God or the good spirit although we may experience the one action of God as an intervention.

The Experience of Being in Tune

The perpetual attraction of such myths as the pursuit of the Holy Grail indicates the depth of the human desire to be in tune with God's intention. These myths touch a chord deep within us which may well be the Spirit of God who dwells in our hearts. The second rule for the discernment of spirits in the *Spiritual Exercises* speaks "of those who go on earnestly striving to cleanse their souls from sin and who seek to rise in the service of God our Lord to greater perfection." In our terminology these are people who desire to attune their actions with the one action of God and desire it effectively. In this case, Ignatius says,

> . . . it is characteristic of the evil spirit to harass with anxiety, to afflict with sadness, to raise obstacles backed by fallacious reasonings that disturb the soul. Thus he seeks to prevent the soul from advancing.
>
> It is characteristic of the good spirit, however, to give courage and strength, consolations, tears, inspirations, and peace. This He does by making all easy, by removing all obstacles so that the soul goes forward in doing good.[11]

Can we make sense of this for our times? If you have ever experienced a time when you were "in the flow," able to live with relative unambivalence and lack of fear in the "now," attuned to the presence of God, then you have an idea of what it might be like to be at one with the one action of God. In such a state you are a contemplative in action. You know that you are at the right place at the right time. There are no doubts about whether you should be someone else or somewhere else. You do not need to justify being married or single or a religious; it is right to be who you are here and now. And you live and act comfortably with the knowledge of your own limitations, of your finitude, of your small part in the immense history of the world. To be attuned to the one action of God, to his will, is to be extraordinarily free, happy and fulfilled even in the midst of a world of sorrow and pain. One can, perhaps, understand how Jesus could celebrate the Last Supper even though he knew in his bones that it would be "last."

In *Gift from the Sea* Anne Morrow Lindbergh likens a good relationship to a dance. It is, she says,

> built on some of the same rules. The partners do not need to hold on tightly, because they move confidently in the same pattern, intricate but gay and swift and free, like a country dance of Mozart's. To touch heavily would be to arrest the pattern and freeze the movement, to

> check the endlessly changing beauty of its unfolding. There is no place here for the possessive clutch, the clinging arm, the heavy hand; only the barest touch in passing. Now arm in arm, now face to face, now back to back—it does not matter which. Because they know they are partners moving to the same rhythm, creating a pattern together, and being invisibly nourished by it.
>
> The joy of such a pattern is not only the joy of creation or the joy of participation, it is also the joy of living in the moment. Lightness of touch and living in the moment are intertwined. One cannot dance well unless one is completely in time with the music, not leaning back to the last step or pressing forward to the next one, but poised directly on the present step as it comes. Perfect poise on the beat is what gives good dancing its sense of ease, of timelessness, of the eternal.[12]

This description of a good relationship seems to fit our experience of God when we are in tune with God's one intention, when we are living as much as possible as brothers and sisters of the Lord Jesus. And the description of being a clumsy dancer seems to fit our experience of God when we are out of tune with God's one intention. Moreover, they strike me as coinciding remarkably well with what Ignatius describes as consolation and desolation and with what Macmurray intends by the subordination of the motive of fear to that of love.

In Tune with the Dance of the Trinity

I am also reminded of the term the Greek Fathers used to describe the mutual indwelling of the three Persons of the Trinity, *Perichoeresis,* which means quite literally, dancing around. We have already noted how theologians say of the three Persons that the only quality that distinguishes them from one another is their mutual relationship. To describe this mutuality of relationships the best metaphor the Greek theologians could come up with was the dance. Quite apart from creation, in other words, the one God is dance, the perfect relationships which we call

Father, Son, Holy Spirit, who are so perfectly related that nothing distinguishes them except their relations. It may even be, as we said earlier, that the pain we feel when we love someone deeply, yet cannot be perfectly one with him or her, is another indication that we are made in the image and likeness of God where such union is the reality.

These lines of Yeats capture some of the same sense of consolation.

> Labor is blossoming or dancing where
> The body is not bruised to pleasure soul,
> Nor beauty born out of its own despair,
> Nor blear-eyed wisdom out of midnight oil.
> O chestnut-tree, great-rooted blossomer,
> Are you the leaf, the blossom or the bole?
> O body swayed to music, O brightening glance,
> How can we know the dancer from the dance?
> (From "Among School Children")

Thus, the experience of God as dance may reflect an encounter with God's one action which is the universe. That is, when our actions are in tune with God's one action with its intention that all human beings live as sisters and brothers, we experience ourselves as in the flow, living in the present with a relative freedom from fear of the future or past, and we address the mysterious Presence that we also encounter as Thou. When our actions are out of tune with God's one action, we experience a malaise, a disharmony, and if we let that disharmony into our consciousness, we know that we need help and we address "a higher Power," as the first step of Alcoholics Anonymous calls God, a Thou by whom alone we can be saved. But in addition, the experience of God as dance may reflect an encounter with God who is, quite apart from creation, the perfect dance, the Mystery who is Three in One.

Consolation

God's will for each of us is not utilitarian; that is, God does not use us for God's own purposes.[13] We are not means to God's end. Rather, if we were able to be perfectly attuned to God's one action, we would be perfectly happy and would also be cocreators of this one action which intends a community of lovers. To the extent that we are in tune, to that extent we are happy and fulfilled and cocreators of that community. This is the satisfactoriness of a way of life which Macmurray says is the justification for that way of life.[14] In a very real sense then, right action (orthopraxis) reveals right belief (orthodoxy) as liberation theology proposes. Jesus also seems to have had this in mind when he said, "Thus, by their fruit you will recognize them" (Mt 7:20). This satisfactoriness of life is, I believe, the consolation described by Ignatius.

> I call it consolation when an interior movement is aroused in the soul, by which it is inflamed with love of its Creator and Lord, and as a consequence, can love no creature on the face of the earth for its own sake, but only in the Creator of them all. It is likewise consolation when one sheds tears that move to the love of God, whether it be because of sorrow for sins, or because of the sufferings of Christ our Lord, or for any other reason that is immediately directed to the praise and service of God. Finally, I call consolation every increase of faith, hope, and love, and all interior joy that invites and attracts to what is heavenly and to the salvation of one's soul by filling it with peace and quiet in its Creator and Lord.[15]

Josef Sudbrack suggests that the modern concept of identity covers inner experiences similar to those of the concept of consolation though without the reference to God.[16] Erikson describes identity as *"an invigorating sameness* and continuity" and indicates that what William James called character in the following letter to his wife means the same as his concept of identity:

> A man's character is discernible in the mental or moral attitude in which, when it came upon him, he felt himself most deeply and intensely active and alive. At such

> moments there is a voice inside which speaks and says: "*This* is the real me!" (Such experience always includes) . . . an element of active tension, of holding my own, as it were, and trusting outward things to perform their part so as to make it a full harmony, but without any *guaranty* that they will. Make it a guaranty . . . and the attitude immediately becomes to my consciousness stagnant and stingless. Take away the guaranty, and I feel . . . a sort of deep enthusiastic bliss, of bitter willingness to do and suffer anything . . . and which, although it is a mere mood or emotion to which I can give no form in words, authenticates itself to me as the deepest principle of all active, and theoretic determination which I possess.[17]

Thus, the best criterion by which to discern God's action in one's life is the sense of a developing inner and outer harmony, a growing sense of one's own self as distinct from and independent of, yet related to, important other people, one's world, one's God.

Since, however, my position in the world is problematic, bedevilled by original sin and its consequences, I am not, *ipso facto*, in tune with the one action of God. I find myself torn between fear and love, between the desire for union and the terror of it. Moreover, I live in a world of conflicting desires, of conflicting groups, of conflicting claims. How can I know how to align myself with the one action of God? This is the point where discernment comes in. If I want to attune my actions and intentions with God's one action and intention, then I must discipline my heart to hear what his intention is, or rather, I must let my heart be disciplined to hear how my actions fit into his one action. I must be willing to start slowly, to let God train my heart as he did Ignatius', through painstaking trial and error, "God treated him at this time just as a schoolmaster treats a child whom he is teaching."[18] I must learn to pay attention to the movements of my heart and mind, to reflect on them wisely and carefully with the help of others, especially my spiritual director, and to test them over time. In this process I must learn two equally difficult and seemingly incompatible attitudes: to trust myself and my reactions and to recognize how easily I can delude myself. Discernment requires that I believe that God will show himself in my experience and that I yet be wary of mindless credulity toward that same experience.

The Process of Discernment

I can begin this process of discernment, this schooling of the heart, at any point in my life. It is never too late, while I am alive, to try to attune my actions with the one action of God because the future is not yet determined and so I can codetermine it in tune with God's intention or not. The door to repentance and conversion is always open. At the same time I have to realize that my actions do create an environment which limits my further action; the past cannot be undone. In the *Spiritual Exercises* Ignatius notes that some people have made an irrevocable election and so are not free to go back on that. Hence, for them he proposes a reformation of life. Even though the irrevocable choice had been made inordinately and was, thus, in Ignatius' eyes not a vocation from God, he saw no way out of valid marriage or ordination.[19] In our day we have seen a loosening of the absoluteness of such choices, but still we need to recognize that major choices in life do have consequences that cannot be undone. This insight leads in two directions. On the one hand, it argues for the seriousness of beginning the schooling of the heart as early as possible so that more of my future can be more fully attuned to God's one action. On the other hand, it counsels us to the wisdom which does not cry over spilt milk, but accepts the reality of the present as the environment where *now* I must seek God's will for the future. Moreover, as we shall presently see, such wisdom must also embrace the limiting environment created by the past actions of others.

The Examination of Consciousness

We can, perhaps, better understand Ignatius' own practice of the examination of conscience as well as his well-known insistence that whatever other spiritual exercises a Jesuit's apostolic labors required him to forego, the examination of conscience twice daily should be retained. Ignatius, apparently, was accustomed to making frequent examinations every day of his life, even long after his period of scruples had passed. I believe that the practice was Ignatius' way of trying to remain in tune with God's action at every moment of his day. For Ignatius each moment and period of the day was, as it were, a period of prayer, a period of walking with the Lord. So he advised periodic reflection on those periods of "prayer." In this way, he hoped, people would become contemplatives in action.

There is a saying attributed to Ignatius which is often totally misinterpreted as: "Pray as if everything depended on God, work as if everything depended on you." In fact, it is loosely translated in just the opposite manner as: "Pray as if everything depended on you, work as if everything depended on God."[20] I pray, that is, I put myself in conscious relationship with God, in order to attune myself to him, to become one with him in intention and action because I do codetermine the future. So the future does depend on me. Paul Claudel, at the head of one of his plays, quotes a Portuguese proverb: "God writes straight with crooked lines." My line can be more or less straight depending on how in tune I am with God's one action. Once I have done my best to get my line straight, then I can work "as if everything depended on God," as indeed it does. I can let God write straight with my crooked line, or with the crooked line which is my action as it meshes with and conflicts with the actions of others. In other words, like Jesus, I do the best I can and leave resurrection to the Father, leave the "success" or "failure" of my actions to the one action of God.

Beyond Individual Discernment

This understanding of discernment pushes beyond the confines of individual discernment. My present environment is not just the product of my own past choices, but of those of many others, and the "success" or "failure" of my intentions depends on the actions of others. The one action of God includes and takes into account not only all these individual actions but also the institutions, processes, and structures which are in some fashion the product of the joint decisions of many individuals both to found them and to keep them in existence. Families, schools, churches, societies, companies, conglomerates of companies, nations are all part of the one action of God which is the universe. These institutions enhance and limit the freedom and agency of individuals and of groups, and they can be more or less in tune with the one action of God, that is, they can foster or inhibit the conditions that lead to community. For example, the communication and economic structures of our modern world make all of us more interdependent and conscious of our interdependence. These structures make possible extraordinary humanitarian efforts to care for people who have been devastated by wars or natural disasters. Hence, they make the community of all people more possible. At the same time, the communication structures reveal to us how inequitable and inimical to community many of the economic structures we take for granted are.

At whatever point of history I act, therefore, I am limited in what is concretely possible by the environment which is the product of the history of the universe, and more specifically of humanity, to that point, as well as by the actions of those who are also acting in that same environment. Even if I want to, I cannot reinvent the wheel, as it were. One example may suffice to illustrate the meaning of this insight for the theory and practice of discernment. The present General of the Society of Jesus does not have the same freedom to discern apostolic directions for the Society of Jesus that Ignatius had, because the almost 450 years since its founding have created a wholly new environment which includes institutional commitments, political and religious alliances and misalliances, and traditions within the Society, as well as a different international and church order that both enhance and constrain what might be done. The present General must do his discerning in this environment. There is no other theater but the present one wherein he can do his part to codetermine the future. The wisdom necessary for discernment requires an acceptance of the present environment as the one and only theater for my action.

These reflections lead us to the issue of communal discernment. Most of the institutions which form our environment are the product of communal decisions or at least of communal acquiescence in their maintenance. More and more we are recognizing our interdependence on one another. What happens in the Persian Gulf affects life in South America and vice-versa. The decision by a mayor and city council to build a subway line through one neighborhood rather than another will affect the lives and actions of people in both neighborhoods, for good or ill. Institutions, laws, projects, and social groupings can be more or less attuned to the one action of God, can create an environment more or less conducive to community building. Moreover, the technological advances of this century face us with the terrifying challenge of harnessing the energies of many of our institutions and structures to be more in harmony with God's one action, or of seeing those energies destroy civilization on our planet. A burning question for our day, therefore, is how to make those institutions and structures more attuned to God's will. Ultimately this question reduces to how to foster among more and more human beings a desire and an ability to discern communally, because only persons can act and only persons can decide to act in concert. There is, perhaps, no greater challenge to religion today than to foster the conditions that make such communal discernment possible.[21]

At the same time we must recognize that there are enormous difficulties in the way of communal discernment. If fear often predominates in relationships between individuals, how much more does it operate in groups and between groups. Moreover, individuals and groups feel more and more powerless to change the conditions of their lives. The power of the state, of the military-industrial complex and of multinational corporations seems overwhelming. Economic, political and social structures seem too complicated and intricate to be changed. If we do not believe in the possibility of effecting change, we will not group together to try to discern communally. It is no accident, I believe, that the flurry of interest in communal discernment in the early 1970's died down. Many people feel the futility of "fighting City Hall," as it were.[22]

And yet there are signs of hope. The basic thrust of the "communidades de base" of Brazil and other parts of South America is to enable groups of ordinary people to trust one another enough to believe in their power to make society, or some part of it, more amenable to gospel values. Rosemary Haughton notes:

> Over the last six years I had been part of a small, new, poor, insecure but obstinately hopeful community of mixed Christians and not-particularly-Christians, trying to help each other to find ways and values to make sense of life now, and to help those damaged by the evils of life now (including their own).

She then goes on to say that in her travels as a lecturer all over North America she "found evidence that people were being drawn together in just such little, unknown, yet obstinately hopeful groups as that from which I came. In country or city, permanently or briefly, people were gathering to live, study, work, pray together."[23] Groups such as these are fostering the conditions that make communal discernment possible. Such efforts are urgently needed at all levels of society and church and throughout the world. More and more of God's people need to believe that the power of love, the drive toward making the one community of all people which God intends, is greater than those powers of this world which seem hell-bent on thwarting the one action of God. Perhaps the greatest sin of our day is not to believe in God's power, the power of love, the power of the Holy Spirit who dwells in our hearts.

Conclusion

That Holy Spirit dwelling in our hearts can be likened to a tuning fork set to the music of God's action. We can become attuned to the one action by becoming more and more aware of the tone played in our hearts by the Holy Spirit. Individually we can attune our actions to that pitch and tone, and by sharing our experience we can become more attuned to the whole range of the music of God's one action. In the sharing of experience we become church in the best sense, a sign of the presence of the Triune God in our midst. But such attunement will not come easily. Humility, asceticism, honesty, and a commitment to prayer, reflection, and communal sharing are absolute necessities. The cacophony that wants to drown out the music of God's one action is loud and insistent. We need to recall what Jesus said about the demon which the apostles could not cast out: "This kind cannot be driven out by anything but prayer" (Mk 9:29). And it may not be amiss to add what other ancient manuscripts add: "and fasting."

7. A Theology of the Ministry of Spiritual Direction

"Whoever has only himself as a guide follows a fool." Good, practical wisdom that applies in many endeavors. But can we not say that the real guide in the spiritual life is the Holy Spirit? Thus, no one has only himself as a guide. However, the tradition has consistently believed that everyone who wants to develop his or her relationship with God needs to seek the help of someone else, even granted that the ultimate spiritual director is the Holy Spirit. Are there theological grounds for this tradition besides the fact of the tradition itself?

Community with the Trinity

Throughout this book we have been developing the thesis that God's intention for our world is an inclusive community of all people in union with the Triune God. Such a community is defined by the ties of friendship that bind individuals to one another. Friendship, however, means that love predominates over fear, and it must be freely given, not coerced. Moreover, friendship means sharing of all that one is and has with one's friends. Friendship is love. In the "Contemplation to Attain the Love of God" which caps *The Spiritual Exercises* Ignatius calls attention to two points:

> 1. The first is that love ought to manifest itself in deeds rather than in words.

> 2. The second is that love consists in a mutual sharing of goods, for example, the lover gives and shares with the beloved what he possesses, or something of that which he has or is able to give; and vice versa, the beloved shares with the lover. Hence, if one has knowledge, he shares it with the one who does not possess it; and so also if one has honors, or riches. Thus, one always gives to the other.[1]

If one always gives to the other, then clearly fear has been cast out or at least put permanently in subordination to love.

The model, of course, is the Triune God in whom the three Persons so completely share all they have and are with one another that they are One. Moreover, God has, without any fear at all, emptied Self in order to become what we are, has freely included what is not God in God's own inner life. In the first point of that same contemplation Ignatius says:

> I will ponder with great affection how much God our Lord has done for me, and how much He has given me of what He possesses, and finally, how much, as far as He can, the same Lord desires to give Himself to me according to His divine decrees.[2]

In these words we can almost feel the poignancy of God's love who cannot give us as much of God's self as God would like both because we are finite and because we are resistant.

Now what God wants to share with us is not so much riches or honor or knowledge, but God's very own interpersonal life. God reveals God's Self, God's values, hopes, dreams, desires and intention. If God is the model of our community life, then what we are asked to share with one another more than anything else are our values, hopes, dreams, desires and intentions. At their deepest level these are, however, our experiences of God. In other words, the community God draws us toward is a religious community. Religious community is not at root defined by any organizational structure, but by a unity of experience.

> The religious community is based on, and at the same time aids in creating, a transindividual *unity of experience*. This unity represents the funded result of many individual experiences and their interpretation which have been shared and compared for the purpose of separating the well-founded experience from that which is evanescent or incidental. The community provides the medium whereby experience passes beyond individual form and becomes more sharply defined in terms of generic and repeatable features.[3]

The religious community God desires is a community of shared experience of God's own community life. Admittedly we are speaking of an ideal, but it is an ideal God wants for us and enables, if we are willing to let God do so. To move toward this ideal we must let the Holy Spirit help us to subordinate our fears to love.

Ministry in the Church

All ministry in the church, I believe, must have as its ultimate aim to facilitate the move toward developing communities of shared experience of God's own community life. Here we have the theological ground for a strong statement in *The Practice of Spiritual Direction*.

> . . . spiritual direction may be considered the core form from which all other forms of pastoral care radiate, since ultimately all forms of pastoral care and counseling aim, or should aim, at helping people to center their lives in the mystery we call God.[4]

In other words, spiritual direction helps people to pay attention to and to share with another member of the community experiences of God, and in the process to learn how to discern what is authentically of God from what is not. In this way they also learn how to talk about their experiences of God with other members of the community. The ministry of spiritual direction, thus, is formative of the religious community God desires.[5]

Uncovering Resistance and Illusion

Because we are limited and sinful people and have unintegrated fears, we can and do resist experiencing the full reality of God's Self-communication. We continually construct idols to which we give the name God. Our images of God-in-relationship-with-us are always skewed by our biases and blind spots and resistances. One could, indeed, describe conversion as a lifelong process of letting God remove the scales from our eyes so that we can more and more embrace the reality of God's overwhelming love for us.[6] In this lifelong process of withdrawal and return we need one another to help us to overcome our resistance to the light. Spiritual directors who themselves recognize both their thirst for God and their resistance to slaking that thirst can help people to move toward more and more reality. John Smith makes an instructive analogy between the scientific community and the religious community.

> In both cases the singular or isolated experience, subject as it is to the possibility of error, receives whatever critical support it is to get from the testimony of other experiences taking place within a unifying community of thought and experience.[7]

Thus, the ministry of spiritual direction helps individuals in the community to come to an ever deeper and more realistic conception of who God is in relationship to us. The community at large is also helped to remain open to the ever greater God who is absolute Mystery and who is always active in helping individuals and the whole community to overcome their biases and blind spots. Humble and honest sharing of experience will keep the community on the move toward the reality of God. Smith astutely notes that the "religious community, unfortunately, has often been reluctant to take seriously the critical force of experience." It has often used authority to maintain itself and ignored the question of whether beliefs can be supported by experience. A "religion which hopes to save its life," he says, "cannot ultimately afford to avoid the critical test of shared experience. On the contrary, from shared experience comes its life."[8] Once again, we see the centrality of the ministry of spiritual direction for the life of the church.

The Ministry of Spiritual Direction

In *The Practice of Spiritual Direction* Connolly and I noted that there is no office or order of spiritual direction in the church.[9] Does this fact follow from the theology we have been developing in this book? I believe so. If the religious community is formed on the basis of shared experience, then people have to share their experience of God with one another. But this is very difficult to do. In order to share the deepest and most sacred part of myself with another person I need to trust that person. It would be foolhardy to entrust myself to a fool or a mountebank; it would be equally foolhardy to entrust myself to someone who gave no indication that he or she would know how to receive what I have to share or how to respond to it. Office in the church does not guarantee such gifts. Indeed, since the church has always known this, it could turn aside as heretical the Donatist thesis that evil and seriously sinful priests could not validly perform sacramental rites. That is, the church held that sacraments performed by such priests did validly convey the grace of God. An evil and heretical priest may validly baptize me, but I would not, unless I were misled, willingly share with him my soul. I would, however, also be loath to share my soul with the underdeveloped priests described in a study of the Roman Catholic priesthood in the United States as the majority of the sample studied.

> The chief area in which underdeveloped priests manifest their lack of psychological growth is in their relationships with other persons. These relationships are ordinarily distant, highly stylized, and frequently unrewarding for the priest and for the other person. . . . It

> is surprising to find in this group of men a general inability to articulate a deep level of personal religious faith.[10]

Obviously ordination does not automatically give one the kind of gifts needed to be a spiritual director.

If the church needs shared experience for its life, then the church needs people whom others can trust. Such people have by grace and training the gifts needed to do the ministry of spiritual direction well.[11] The ministry of spiritual direction is a charism in the church. People who have the charism are almost naturally grateful and humble before the gift. Moreover, they find their deepest fulfillment in listening to the experiences of God which others entrust to them. At the risk of some irreverence, I want to note that spiritual directors need to have the kind of gratitude predicated of a helpful psychoanalyst in Salinger's short story *Franny and Zooey.* Their mother is talking to Zooey about his sister Franny's need of a psychoanalyst. Zooey tells his mother:

> For a psychoanalyst to be any good with Franny at all, he'd have to be a pretty peculiar type. I don't know. He'd have to believe that it was through the grace of God that he'd been inspired to study psychoanalysis in the first place. He'd have to believe that it was through the grace of God that he wasn't run over by a goddam truck before he ever even got his license to practice. He'd have to believe that it's through the grace of God that he has the native intelligence to be able to help his goddam patients at *all.* I don't know any *good* analysts who think along those lines. But that's the only kind of psychoanalyst who might be able to do Franny any good at all.[12]

Throughout the church's history God has raised up men and women of grateful hearts who have themselves developed relations of intimacy with God. In the Egyptian desert abbas (fathers) and ammas (mothers) "became known for their holiness and spiritual wisdom, their knowledge of the heart," and were sought out by people looking for something "more" in their lives.

> This spiritual mentoring included both the acknowledgment of sin and the discernment of God's spirit in the heart, a form of lay confession, since those consulted were most often not ordained. They believed . . . that the opening of one's heart to another, what they called *exagoreusis*, leads to *hesychia* or peace of heart.[13]

This practice was brought to Ireland after its conversion and became the tradition of *anamchara* or soul friend. Again in Ireland the reputation for holiness and wisdom led to choice of the soul friend, and again lay women and men were sought as soul friends. In our own day God continues to raise up such grateful kinds of people who are deeply interested in knowing God and who, as a result of that interest and their own listening skills, win the trust of those people who want to know and love God with all their hearts, with all their minds and with all their strength. Of course, throughout history the ultimate soul friend is God, but we all need the mediating help of others as well.

The Community Needed for Effective Ministry

Throughout this book we have also noted that all of our relationships, whether with the three Persons in God or with other human beings, are problematic. All of us have unintegrated fears which keep us from community with God and with one another. All ministry, we have indicated, is aimed at helping people to overcome their fears so that love and the community love intends can prevail. In the rest of this chapter I want to speak of the community of relationships necessary for any ministry in the church.

The Minister's Need for a Personal Relationship with God

If all ministry in the church has as its ultimate aim to facilitate the development of community relationships with the Trinity, then we need to take seriously the words of Jesus: "Can one blind man guide another? Surely both will fall into a pit? . . . Hypocrite! Take the plank out of your own eye first, and then you will see clearly enough to take out the splinter that is in your brother's eye" (Lk 6:39–42). Applied to the present topic Jesus' words translate into a command to ministering people to work on their own relationship with God before they try to help others. The development of a relationship, however, does not come about in any other way than by engaging in it. For too long divinity schools, seminaries, and formation programs seemed to operate on the assumption that sound theology was all that a minister needed. Again, just as I do not wish to disparage sound psychology, so too, I am not disparaging sound theology. After all, this book is based on the premise that a sound theology is helpful for ministry. Reading a good book about marriage may help a couple, but it does not spare them the pains and joys of actually relating. Likewise, a sound course on God may help a minister, but it cannot take the place of engaging God in relationship. Thus, if I am to help others with their relationship with God, I must have developed my own relationship. Else I will deserve the epithet, "Hypocrite!"

Here is a simple diagram of that relationship. The arrow pointing both ways indicates that the relationship is mutual and dialogical. God communicates (reveals) Godself, and the minister does the same. As we have already noted, on our side the relationship is problematic. Unintegrated fears hinder our openness to God, both our openness to God's Self-revelation and our own willingness and ability to reveal ourselves. We need something that will hold us in the relationship when the fears grow strong, and that "something" is a foundational experience of

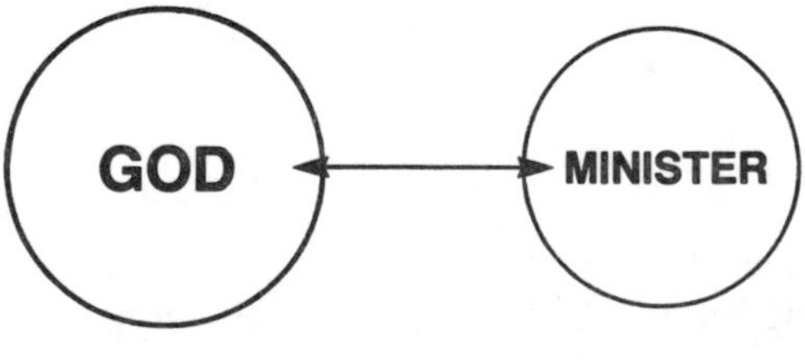

God's creative love. What experience will ground and forge such a strong enough bond with God? I believe that it is the experience of being created out of love of which we spoke in chapter 2, the welling up of desire for "I know not what."

The Minister's Need for Spiritual Direction

However, as we noted in chapter 5, the rhythm of withdrawal and return is a lifelong process. Our resistances to God can be very strong and determined. The sources can be our distorted images of God and of ourselves, for example, our poor self-image. The sources can also be whatever it is deep within us that cannot brook awareness of finitude, limitation, and death. Nor should we neglect the Evil One and his minions as sources of resistance. Thus, because of the strength and determination of these resistances, people throughout history who sought to develop a more intimate relationship with God have been advised to seek help. Traditionally that help has been called spiritual direction. Another relationship enters the diagram.

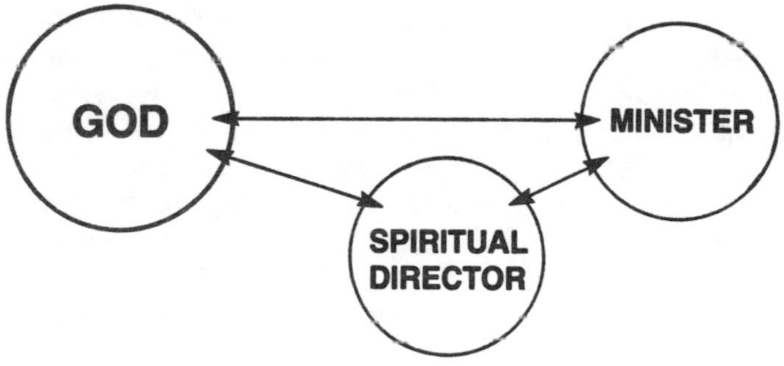

The Spiritual Director's Needs

Spiritual directors take it as their central task to help people to develop their relationship with God and to live out the consequences of that relationship, as we have repeatedly stated. They enter into a deep relationship with those whom they direct in order to serve the latters' relationship with God. But the injunction of Jesus recurs here; spiritual directors will be blind guides unless they, too, engage the Lord directly. So we have added the arrow that indicates the mutual relationship of director and God. Since that relationship will also be problematic, the spiritual director needs a director of his/her own. Already we can see that the diagram can be extended indefinitely along that line. Obviously a community of relationships is already being established and all of them center in God.

The Need for Supervision

I want to complicate the diagram in another direction, however. Not only are the relationships between the minister and God and between the spiritual director and God problematic, but the relationship between the minister and the spiritual director is problematic, and here from both sides. That is, both the minister and the director have unintegrated fears that can get in the way of the purpose of their relationship. The minister who is the directee can develop transference reactions to the director, and it is the work of the director not to let these get too much in the way of their working alliance (which is to help the directee's relationship with God). But the director is also a human being and can develop distortions (countertransference reactions) toward the directee.[14] Moreover, the very act of listening to another's experiences of God may trigger in the director resistances to God and lead to harmful interactions with the directee. How can a director get help? First of all, through his/her own relationship with God and with a spiritual director. Secondly, through individual or group supervision which introduces another level of complexity to our diagram.

Supervision, as distinct from consultation, focuses on the experiences of the spiritual director in his/her work with directees.[15] The supervisor helps the director to look at that experience and make sense of it in the light of the director's own psychological and spiritual dynamics. Once again we must note that supervisors can be the blind leading the blind unless they, too, are engaged in the multiple relationships already indicated for directors, most especially the relationship with God. The

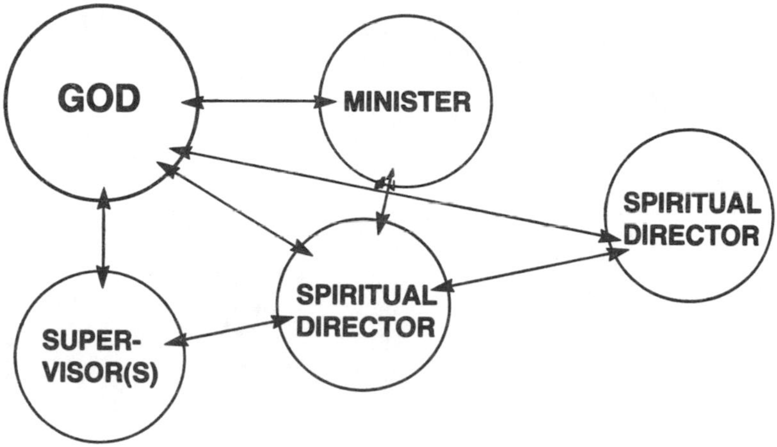

community threatens to become infinite. And why not? Is that not exactly what God wants, a universal community of brothers and sisters of the Lord Jesus, all of whom love and care for one another because they are in communion with God and all of whom can share with one another their experience of God?

The Faith Community

Finally, the minister in the diagram actually ministers; that is, he/she enters ministerial relationships with groups (a congregation, for example) or individuals with the purpose of helping them with their relationship with God. (It should be noted that ministers, spiritual directors, and supervisors do not create the relationship with God; they help people to develop a relationship that already exists because God intends it.) Here is how the diagram now looks, but I have tried to indicate that God is not one being among other beings by including all the relationships within the immensity of a circle and making all the individual or group relations to God converge on the center of the circle. Note that I have added the possibility of a supervisor for the minister. (It would complicate the diagram unnecessarily to add the relationships of the supervisors to their own spiritual directors

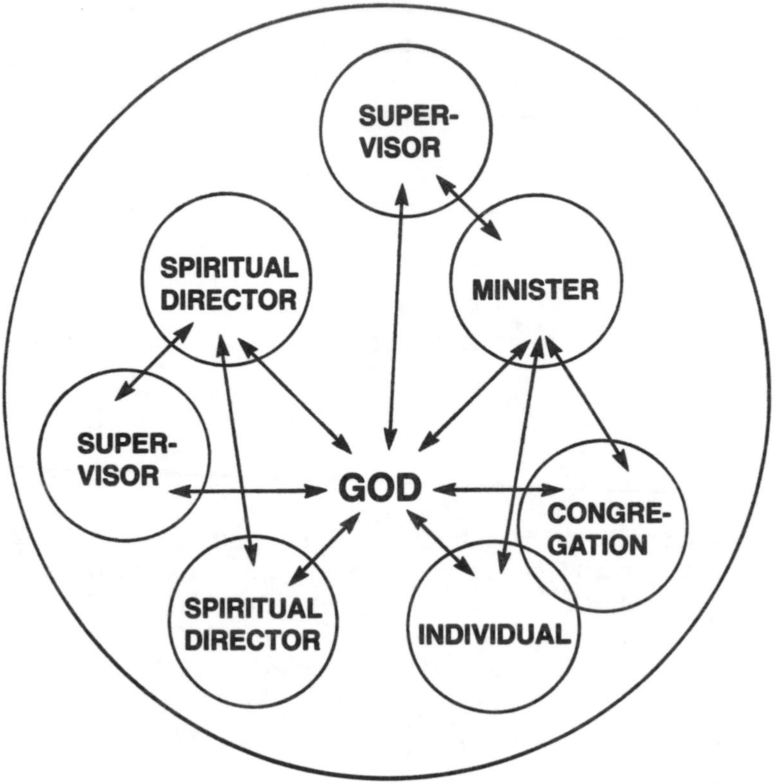

and supervisors. But those relationships are implied in the model we are developing.) If we recall that each of the individuals has multiple relationships that all lead back to or come from God, then we can see how complex a series of interrelationships any one minister has. And all of them are problematic because of unintegrated fear, yet all of them are embraced in the universal love of God whose Spirit is poured forth into our hearts. And perfect love can cast out fear, as the First Letter of John tells us. Each of the relationships that make up this community of believers tries to enable openness of communication about the central mystery of all our lives, a loving divine community which wants each of us to live with our fears subordinated to our love of God and one another.

The training of ministers has been pervaded by the insights of psychiatry, psychology, and social work. Ministry has been enhanced greatly by these insights and training procedures. If, however, we fail to move beyond psychology and into the heart of ministry itself in our ministerial training programs, we will, I believe, fail to help aspiring ministers to remove the plank from their own eyes with the consequence of ministerial malpractice. Training programs must foster the development of these mutual relationships of trust. All of these relationships may not be necessary throughout one's ministerial career, but all of them are needed in the early going, and some of them may be dropped later only at one's peril and the peril of the people of God. The one relationship which cannot be allowed to stagnate in the minister, whatever the length of service, is the one with the Mystery we call God. Hence, we had better start working on that one as early in the process as possible.

Some Practical Suggestions

For those seeking spiritual direction. While it is possible to use the search for the "perfect" director as a way to resist getting any direction, still, I would urge some practical cautions. In seeking a director do not be afraid to ask what kind of experience and training a director has had. If the director gets huffy and defensive, go somewhere else. The novel, *Glittering Images*, provides a fine example of openness by a potential director. Dr. Ashworth has just found out that his spiritual director is dead and is hesitating about entrusting himself to the new Abbot, Jon Darrow. Darrow says:

> Let me tell you a little about myself. . . . I think it's often difficult to confide in someone new and untried; spiritual directors are not, after all, something one acquires without thought at the local shop, like a sack of potatoes. I'm fifty-seven years old and I entered the Order when I was forty-three. Before that I was a chaplain in the prison service, and before that I was a chaplain in the Navy—in which, incidentally, I served during the War. I obtained my theology degree at Laud's.

> For nine years of my life I was a married man and I have a son and daughter, now grown up. . . That, I fear, is very much of a thumbnail sketch, but I hope perhaps you may find it illuminating.[16]

If the director, like Abbot Darrow, non-defensively tells you about the extent of his/her experience and admits limitations and hesitations, ask whether he/she sees a spiritual director currently. If the answer is negative, you might ask whether the director is willing to say why. It could be that he/she has had direction regularly and has decided with his/her director that it is not needed for now. You might also ask whether the director sees a supervisor or is involved in peer supervision or has done so in the past. Even though you are asking the other for help, you have a right to know something about the prospective helper. Spiritual directors who trust only themselves and their own relationship with God, who do not seek spiritual direction or supervision for themselves, can do a lot of harm. *Caveat emptor.* Let the buyer beware (even if there is no fee for direction).[17]

For those who seek supervision. Supervision of spiritual direction is still in its early adolescence. As a result, there are not many trained supervisors around. At present it is often a question of pulling ourselves up by our own bootstraps. In asking for individual or group supervision try to keep the focus of the supervision on the experience of the one(s) present, not on directees. Supervision is different from consultation. In the latter the focus might be on the absent person; in supervision the focus is on the experience of the director who is present, on the director's experience of doing the ministry of direction. The purpose is to help the director to become a better director by looking at and trying to understand his/her reactions and behavior while engaging in the ministry of spiritual direction.[18]

Conclusion

In this chapter we have drawn out the implications of the theology we have developed in the earlier chapters for an understanding of the ministry of spiritual direction. Because the church is a community of shared experience, it needs the ministry of a kind of spiritual direction which helps people to pay attention to the religious dimension of their experience and to share it with the spiritual director. As more and more of God's people share their experience of God with one another, we will move toward the community God intends, a community where fear is subordinated to love and which is in principle inclusive of every human being in the world.

8. Conclusion

In his *Confessions* Augustine said to God: "You have made us for Yourself, and our hearts are restless until they rest in You." When we experience that restlessness, that desire for "we know not what," we experience the one intention of God in creating this universe. The perfect community which is the one God, Father, Word and Spirit, is creating this universe for one reason and with one motive. The motive is superabundant, freely given love, the reason or intention that all persons join the community of the Trinity. Thus, at the heart of the universe is the creative desire of God to draw us into the universal community whose motive is love and whose intention is community.

God works continually to convince each one of us that God's community life is our greatest boon. Moreover, God wants us to create institutions and structures and laws that will make this community life more possible for all persons. The aim of all ministry in the church, therefore, must be to make it more possible for us to pay attention to and to carry out the deepest desire of our hearts, namely, to live in community with the Trinity and with one another.

Our theological inquiry has been leading us to this conclusion. For me to have undertaken the inquiry and for you, the reader, to have undertaken the journey with me the only motive could have been the love of God poured out into our hearts by the Holy Spirit whom he has given us (cf. Rom 5:5). In effect, this whole inquiry has been impelled by the kind of desire voiced by Anselm of Canterbury as he began his own theological inquiry in his *Proslogion* and which we cited in the first chapter.

> Teach us to seek You, and reveal Yourself to us as we seek; for unless You instruct us we cannot seek You, and unless You reveal Yourself we cannot find You. Let us seek You in desiring You; let us desire You in seeking You. Let us find You in loving You; let us love You in finding You.[1]

The very act of undertaking this theological inquiry, therefore, derives from the desire of God at the heart of the universe.

At every moment of our existence we encounter this creative presence of God, but we are only intermittently aware of the encounter. Ministry in the church must help us to become more and more aware of the reality of this universe. We have seen, however, that our unawareness derives not only from our finiteness but also from our unintegrated fears which lead to our blind spots and resistances to the drawing love of God. These resistances are deep-seated and lead to a lifelong pattern of withdrawal and return in our relationship with God and with one another. Ministry in the church needs to help us to discern what is for our peace and for the peace of the whole world. Gradually we must learn that there is, ultimately, nothing to be afraid of for those who are united with God; we must let perfect love drive out fear (1 Jn 4:18). As we do so, we shall band together with others to create the kind of communities God desires, and we shall not let the powers of this world hinder us from seeking to build such inclusive communities which ultimately intend to be the one universal community which is the Kingdom of God preached by Jesus Christ.

Because our unintegrated fears were learned very early in life, they will not easily be subordinated to love. Hence, we need to help one another. The "golden rule" needs to become our rallying cry as we recognize how far each one of us falls short of God's hopes and dreams. In the final analysis, however, the demons of our fears will only be cast out by prayer (cf. Mk 9:29). Ignatius of Loyola had a great devotion to the Blessed Trinity. In the fragments of his spiritual diary which have been preserved we hear him repeatedly asking the Trinity for confirmation, i.e., for assurance that he was on the right path as he wrote the section of his *Constitutions* on poverty. Over and over he prayed: "Eternal Father, confirm me! Eternal Son, confirm me. Eternal Holy Spirit, confirm me. Holy Trinity, confirm me. My One and Only god, confirm me."[2] We can make this prayer our own as we beg the Holy Trinity to help us to subordinate our fears to the love of God poured out into our hearts. Finally, we want to be able to say and mean the favorite prayer of Francis Xavier, Ignatius' beloved companion, the prayer with which we began this work and with which we shall now end it.

O Deus, Ego Amo Te

O God, I love thee, I love thee—
Not out of hope of heaven for me
Nor fearing not to love and be
  In the everlasting burning.
Thou, thou, my Jesus, after me
  Didst reach thine arms out dying,
For my sake sufferedst nails and lance,
Mocked and marrèd countenance,
  Sorrows passing number,
  Sweat and care and cumber,
Yea and death, and this for me,
  And thou couldst see me sinning:
Then I, why should not I love thee,
Jesu so much in love with me?
Not for heaven's sake; not to be
Out of hell by loving thee;
Not for any gains I see;
But just the way that thou didst me
I do love and I will love thee:
What must I love thee, Lord, for then?—
For being my king and God. Amen.

Gerard Manley Hopkins, S.J.

Annotated Bibliography

Barry, William A., *Paying Attention to God: Discernment in Prayer.* Notre Dame, IN: Ave Maria Press, 1990. Touches on some of the themes of this book.

———. *"Now Choose Life": Conversion as the Way to Life.* New York/Mahwah: Paulist, 1990. Develops the theme of conversion as a lifelong process of moving from illusion to the embrace of reality.

Barry, William A. and Connolly, William J., *The Practice of Spiritual Direction.* San Francisco: Harper & Row (Seabury), 1982. The book which gave rise to the desire for a more developed theology of the encounter with God and of the ministry of spiritual direction.

Fischer, Kathleen, *Women at the Well: Feminist Perspectives on Spiritual Direction.* New York/Mahwah: Paulist, 1988. Looks at the relationship with God and the ministry of spiritual direction from a feminist point of view.

Fleming, David L. (ed.), *The Christian Ministry of Spiritual Direction.* St. Louis: Review for Religious, 1988. A collection of the best articles on spiritual direction from the *Review for Religious.*

Liebert, Elizabeth, *Making Life Choices.* New York/Mahwah: Paulist, in press. Uses structural developmental psychology to illumine the work of spiritual direction.

Ruffing, Janet, *Uncovering Stories of Faith: Spiritual Direction and Narrative.* New York/Mahwah: Paulist, 1989. Develops a theory of spiritual direction through the study of the structure of narrative.

Studzinski, Raymond, *Spiritual Direction and Midlife Development.* Chicago: Loyola University Press, 1985. A helpful review of the psychology of midlife with reference to spiritual direction.

Notes

1. Introduction

[1]For an exhaustive study of the history of spiritual direction cf. "Direction spirituelle," *Dictionnaire de Spiritualité,* Vol. 3 (Paris: Beauchesne, 1957). For shorter histories cf. Kenneth Leech, *Soul Friend: The Practice of Christian Spirituality* (New York: Harper & Row, 1980); Janet Ruffing, *Uncovering Stories of Faith: Spiritual Direction and Narrative.* New York/Mahwah: Paulist, 1989.

[2]William A. Barry and William J. Connolly, *The Practice of Spiritual Direction.* San Francisco: Harper & Row (Seabury), 1982 (hereafter cited as *Practice*).

[3]David L. Fleming, "Spiritual Direction: Charism and Ministry," in David L. Fleming, ed., *The Christian Ministry of Spiritual Direction* (St. Louis, MO: Review for Religious, 1988), 3–9.

[4]Barry and Connolly, *Practice,* 8.

[5]Nancy C. Ring, *America,* Dec. 24, 1983, 417.

[6]Bernard Pitaud, "La direction spirituelle: Propos sur un livre récent," *Christus,* 37, no. 145 (Jan. 1990), 95–102.

[7]John Macmurray, *The Self as Agent.* Atlantic Highlands, NJ: Humanities Press, 1991, 15.

[8]*Anselm of Canterbury. Volume I.* Ed. and tr. by Jaspar Hopkins and Herbert Richardson. Toronto and New York: Edwin Mellen Press, 1974, 92.

2. Understanding God's Presence in the World

[1]Cf. William A. Barry, *"Seek My Face:" Prayer as Personal Relationship in Scripture*. New York and Mahwah, NJ: Paulist, 1989, 17–22.

[2]For empirical studies of the affirmation of experiences of God cf. Alister Hardy, *The Spiritual Nature of Man: A Study of Contemporary Religious Experience* (Oxford: Clarendon Press, 1979) and Andrew M. Greeley, *The Religious Imagination* (New York: Sadlier, 1981).

[3]The Gifford lectures were originally published in two volumes by Faber & Faber of London in 1957 and 1961 and have since been reprinted by Humanities Press. The overall title of the two volumes is *The Form of the Personal*. The two volumes are: John Macmurray, *The Self as Agent* (hereafter cited as *Agent*) and *Persons in Relation* (hereafter cited as *Persons*). Atlantic Highlands, NJ: Humanities Press, 1991.

[4]*Agent, op. cit.*, 71. In *At the Origins of Modern Atheism* Michael Buckley makes a similar point. "Descartes and Malebranche, Newton and Clarke generated a tradition in a way that neither Bruno nor Spinoza did. These theistic traditions finally generated their own denials." (New Haven and London: Yale University Press, 1987), 33.

[5]*Agent*, 90–91.

[6]*Agent*, 134.

[7]*The Autobiography of St. Ignatius Loyola*. Tr. Joseph F. O'Callaghan. Ed. John C. Olin. New York: Harper & Row, 1974, 31.

[8]Cf. Erik K. Erikson, *Childhood and Society,* 2nd. ed. New York: Norton, 1963.

[9]*Agent,* Chapter X. The World as One Action.

[10]*Agent,* 220.

[11]*Agent,* 221.

[12]I might also add that Macmurray thus puts belief at the heart of the philosophical enterprise, making himself a kindred spirit to Karl Rahner in *Hearers of the Word.* New York: Herder & Herder, 1969.

[13]*Persons,* 222.

[14]In *Search for Reality in Religion* (London: Quaker Home Service, 1965) Macmurray writes in a footnote: "The highest, richest and rarest qualities in our experience of human personality, such as creative spontaneity, provide the most adequate basis for our characterization of God. Even these, of course, are inadequate, and we have to use them mythologically. God is beyond the personal, of course; but it is the personal in our experience which points in the direction of God, and provides the most adequate language we possess for references to God" (p. 45, n. 1). In *At the Origins of Modern Atheism* Michael Buckley makes a similar point. *Op. cit.,* 346.

[15]*The Autobiography of St. Ignatius Loyola, op. cit.,* 50.

[16]Stephen W. Hawking, *A Brief History of Time: From the Big Bang to Black Holes.* Toronto, New York, London, Sydney, Auckland: Bantam, 1988, 171.

[17]*Ibid.,* 174.

[18]*Ibid.,* 175.

[19]*Persons*, 169.

[20]Cf. William A. Barry, *Paying Attention to God: Discernment in Prayer.* Notre Dame, IN: Ave Maria, 1990, 77–85.

3. The Religious Dimension of Experience

[1]William James, *The Varieties of Religious Experience: A Study in Human Nature.* New York: Mentor Books, 1958, 367–368. This classic was also originally delivered as the Gifford Lectures around the turn of the century.

[2]Cf. Walter H. Clark, H. Newton Maloney, James Daane, and Alan R. Tippett, *Religious Experience: Its Nature and Function in the Human Psyche.* Springfield, IL: Charles C. Thomas, 1973.

[3]John E. Smith, *Experience and God.* New York: Oxford, 1968.

[4]*Ibid.*, 24.

[5]Cf. John Macmurray, *Idealism Against Religion.* London: Lindsey Press, 1944.

[6]Smith, *op. cit.*, 23.

[7]Bernard J. Lonergan, *Method in Theology.* New York: Herder & Herder, 1972, 15.

[8]Martin Thornton, *My God: A Reappraisal of Normal Religious Experience.* London: Hodder & Stoughton, 1974, 45.

[9]Thomas S. Kuhn, in *The Structure of Scientific Revolutions* (Chicago: University of Chicago Press, 1962), notes that western astronomers did not see new stars (which Chinese astronomers were seeing) until after the Copernican revolution. According to the Ptolemaic theory the heavens were fixed and so no new stars were expected.

[10]John Macmurray makes this point while demonstrating an error in Wittgenstein's initial statement (in *Tractatus Logico-Philosophicus*) that "the world is everything that is the case." "The world contains, no doubt, everything that is the case, but it contains also everything that appears to be the case and is not. Error, stupidity and evil; the illusions of the wishful thinker and the 'nonsense' of the metaphysician, are in the world; and any conception of the world which excludes them is an inadequate conception. It is of no avail to say that all these are only in us, and not in the world. If these are in us, we are in the world, and our stupidities and illusions play their part in determining the history of the world." *Persons, op. cit.*, 219.

[11]*Persons*, 222.

[12]Smith, *op. cit.*, 35.

[13]*Ibid.*, 69.

[14]Karl Rahner, *Spiritual Exercises.* Tr. Kenneth Baker. New York: Herder & Herder, 1965, 248–249.

[15]Frederick Buechner, *The Sacred Journey.* San Francisco: Harper & Row, 1982, 52.

[16]*Ibid.*, 56. Another example comes from the psychoanalytic perspective. William Meissner, without in any way denying the religious dimension, shows in convincing fashion some of the possible elements of the psychological dimension of Ignatius of Loyola's conversion experience. Cf. W. W. Meissner, "Psychoanalytic Hagiography: The Case of Ignatius of Loyola," *Theological Studies* 52 (1991), 3–33.

[17]Cf. C. S. Lewis, *Surprised by Joy: The Shape of My Early Life.* New York: Harcourt, Brace, 1955.

[18]Smith's argument cannot, I believe, be wholly sustained. By the very act of creating us God touches us immediately. We do immediately encounter God. But our experience of the encoun-

ter is always mediated through our bodily sensations, images, memories and thoughts, etc. Separating what is the immediate encounter with God from the media through which it is experienced is matter for discernment. Perhaps Ignatius was touching on this difficulty when after having affirmed the reality of "consolation without cause" he later cautions the one who has had it to be careful about the moments following it. Cf. *The Spiritual Exercises of St. Ignatius*. Tr. Louis J. Puhl. Chicago: Loyola University Press, 1951, n. 336.

[19]Smith, *op. cit.*, 81.

[20]Etty Hillesum, *An Interrupted Life: The Diaries of Etty Hillesum 1941–1943*. New York: Washington Square Press, 1985.

[21]Cf. John Main, *The Heart of Creation* (London: Darton, Longman and Todd, 1988) and M. Basil Pennington, *Centering Prayer: Renewing an Ancient Christian Prayer Form*. Garden City, NY: Doubleday, 1980.

[22]Chapters 6 and 10 of *The Practice of Spiritual Direction* describe at some length the psychological structures called "object relations schemata" that condition all our interpersonal experiences and hence also our experience of God.

[23]Macmurray allows that Freud's assertion that religion is a projection of the child's experience of family life must be accepted, but that such acceptance does not lead to the conclusion that religion is illusory. He turns Freud's argument on its head in this fashion: "The wish to destroy the father and take his place is one of the common phantasies of childhood. Would it not be as good an argument as Freud's, then, if we were to conclude that adult atheism was the projection upon the universe of *this* childish phantasy." *Persons*, 155.

[24]Sebastian Moore, *Let This Mind Be In You: The Quest for Identity Through Oedipus to Christ*. Minneapolis/Chicago/New York: Winston/ Seabury, 1985.

[25]Cf. Alister Hardy, *The Spiritual Nature of Man: A Study of Contemporary Religious Experience*. Oxford: Clarendon Press, 1979.

[26]Hardy, *ibid.*, 20.

[27]*Ibid.*, 21.

[28]*Ibid.*, 76–77.

[29]*Ibid.*, 34.

[30]*Ibid.*, 57.

[31]Smith, *op. cit.*, 35.

[32]*The Autobiography of St. Ignatius Loyola*. Tr. Joseph F. O'Callaghan. Ed. John C. Olin. New York: Harper & Row, 1974, 93.

[33]"Consciousness" is the term George Aschenbrenner prefers to "conscience." Cf. "Consciousness Examen," *Review for Religious*, 1972, 31, 14–21. Reprinted in David L. Fleming (Ed.) *Notes on the Spiritual Exercises of St. Ignatius of Loyola*. St. Louis, MO: Review for Religious, 1983, 175–185.

[34]Cf. "Contemplation to Attain the Love of God," *Spiritual Exercises*, nos. 230–237.

[35]The phrase comes from the title of Peter Berger's book, *A Rumor of Angels: Modern Society and the Rediscovery of the Supernatural*. Garden City, NY: Doubleday Anchor, 1970.

[36]Frans Jozef van Beeck entitles his projected, three-volume systematic theology *God Encountered*. The first volume has appeared, *Understanding the Christian Faith*. San Francisco: Harper & Row, 1989.

4. A Theology of Trinity and of Community

[1]Karl Rahner, "Remarks on the Dogmatic Treatise 'De Trinitate,' " *Theological Investigations IV.* Tr. Kevin Smyth. Baltimore: Helicon Press, 1966, 87.

[2]*Ibid.*, 79.

[3]William A. Barry, *God and You: Prayer As a Personal Relationship*. New York and Mahwah, NJ: Paulist, 1987, 68.

[4]*Ibid.*, 69.

[5]*Persons*, 17.

[6]*Persons*, 24.

[7]*Persons*, 24.

[8]For a thorough overview of Trinitarian theology cf. William J. Hill, *Three-Personed God: The Trinity as a Mystery of Salvation*. Washington, D.C.: Catholic University of America Press, 1982.

[9]It has been a common teaching of theologians that any one of the three divine Persons could have become human. For this thesis they rely on the principle that all three Persons have the same divine power. Rahner raises a serious objection to such a thesis. In the Trinity the personal is what distinguishes the three Persons. They are distinguished by their relations to one another, and by nothing else. Hence we cannot argue from what one Person is to what any one of the them could be. All we know is that the second Person is human; we do not know whether or not the Father or the Spirit could have become human. Cf. Rahner, *op. cit*.

[10]John J. O'Donnell, *The Mystery of the Triune God*. New York/ Mahwah: Paulist, 1989, 119–120.

[11]*Ibid.*, 87.

[12]*Ibid.*, 88. For a wonderful development of the doctrine of Exchange (the *admirabile commercium*) see Rosemary Haughton, *The Passionate God.* London: Darton, Longman and Todd, 1981.

[13]*Ibid.*, 88.

[14]*Ibid.*, 125.

[15]*Persons*, 68.

[16]Cf. Elizabeth Kübler-Ross, *On Death and Dying*. New York, Macmillan, 1969.

[17]*Persons*, 159.

[18]*Persons*, 150.

[19]*Persons*, 157–58.

[20]*Persons*, 163.

[21]Robert Bellah and his associates have shown that individualism is threatening to destroy American civilization. On our analysis individualism leads to a society based on law. Bellah *et al.* argue forcefully that we must develop a language of community and of commitment to one another. They make the case for the necessity of communities of memory, groups who share a tradition and present experience and celebrate both. Cf. Robert Bellah *et al.*, *Habits of the Heart*. New York: Harper & Row, 1985.

[22]John Macmurray, *Search for Reality in Religion.* London: Quaker Home Service, 1984, 64.

[23]*Op. cit.*

[24]In a Lenten series of talks on the BBC in 1964 John Macmurray showed that for Jesus "fear" is the opposite of "faith." Macmurray argues forcefully that Jesus' message was never so critically needed for our world as at present. And, he noted, for all their obvious imperfections the Christian churches are moving toward unity. But the unity must be "a free unity in a bond of trust and affection, through which fear is overcome. It must give us a church which is not on the defensive and has learned how to exist not for its members, but for the world." *To Save from Fear.* Philadelphia: Wider Quaker Fellowship, 1990, 12.

5. The Development of the Relationship with God

[1]*Persons,* 171.

[2]Cf. Erik H. Erikson, *Childhood and Society.* 2nd. ed., rev. and enl. New York: Norton, 1964.

[3]Cf. William A. Barry, "The Experience of the First and Second Weeks of the *Spiritual Exercises,*" *Review for Religious* 32 (1973), 102–109; "On Asking God to Reveal Himself in the *Spiritual Exercises,*" *Review for Religious* 37 (1978), 171–176. Also found in David Fleming, ed., *Notes on the Spiritual Exercises.* St. Louis: Review for Religious, 1983, 95–102, 72–77. Cf. also William A. Barry, *Finding God in All Things: A Companion to the Spiritual Exercises of St. Ignatius.* Notre Dame, IN: Ave Maria, 1991.

[4]Cf. *The Spiritual Exercises of St. Ignatius, op. cit.,* no. 23 and Barry, *Finding God in All Things, op. cit.*

[5]J. S. Mackenzie, *Nervous Disorders and Character.* Cited in Henry Guntrip, *Psychotherapy and Religion.* New York: Harper, 1957, 200.

[6]Peter Faber, *Mémorial.* Traduit et Commenté par Michel de Certeau. Collection Christus, no. 4. Textes. Paris: Desclée de Brouwer, 1960.

[7]Cf. Barry and Connolly, *op. cit.*, Chapter 6, "Development of Relationship and Resistance."

[8]Susan Howatch, *Glittering Images*. New York: Fawcett Crest, 1987, 199.

[9]In the *Spiritual Exercises* Ignatius speaks of this period as the "first week" of the Exercises.

[10]In *To Save From Fear* Macmurray confesses that he feels some depression when he contemplates how far the Christian churches are from what Jesus desired. But then he says, "Such depression, however, is itself fear and [lack of faith]." *Op. cit.*, 12.

[11]In *Christian Conversion: A Developmental Interpretation of Autonomy and Surrender* Walter E. Conn develops in great detail a theory of a fourfold conversion which is based on the theology of Bernard Lonergan and the developmental psychologies of Erikson, Kohlberg, Piaget, and others. The stages of conversion are named moral, affective, cognitive, and religious conversion. Religious conversion means to embrace the fullness of the reality of this world. In a later article Joann Wolski Conn and Walter E. Conn illustrate each stage of conversion in the lives of St. Thérèse of Lisieux and Thomas Merton. Cf. "Discerning Conversion," *The Way Supplement*, Spring, 1989, no. 64, 63–79. I have sketched out the pathway of conversion from illusion to reality in *"Now Choose Life:" Conversion as the Way to Life*. New York/ Mahwah: Paulist, 1990.

[12]Sebastian Moore, *Christ the Liberator of Desire*. New York: Crossword, 1989, 57.

[13]I have explored this source of resistance in a series of articles in *Review for Religious* now published in *Getting to Know God: Prayer and Discernment in Today's Church*. Notre Dame, IN: Ave Maria Press, 1990, Chapters 4, 5, and 6.

[14]Gerald G. May, "The Psychodynamics of Spirituality: A Follow-up." *The Journal of Pastoral Care,* 1977, 31, 87.

6. A Theology of Discernment of Spirits

[1]In his Pulitzer Prize winning book, *The Denial of Death* (New York: Free Press, 1973) Ernest Becker argues persuasively that the fear, indeed, the terror of death lies at the heart of the ills of modern culture.

[2]John Macmurray, *Freedom in the Modern World.* London: Faber & Faber, 1968, 52–53.

[3]*Ibid.*, 24.

[4]*Ibid.*, 53.

[5]*Ibid.*, 146.

[6]*Ibid.*, 147.

[7]C. S. Lewis, *The Pilgrim's Regress: An Allegorical Apology for Christianity, Reason and Romanticism.* New York: Sheed & Ward, 1944, 7–10.

[8]*Freedom in the Modern World, op. cit.*, 147.

[9]For a very cogent argument for the use of the mind in discernment see Michael J. O'Sullivan, "Trust Your Feelings, But Use Your Head," *Studies in the Spirituality of Jesuits,* 22/4 (Sept. 1990).

[10]*Spiritual Exercises, op. cit.*, n. 314.

[11]*Ibid.*, n. 315.

[12]Anne Morrow Lindbergh, *Gift From the Sea.* New York: Vintage Books, 1965, 104–105.

[13]Cf. William A. Barry, "God's Love Is Not Utilitarian," *Review for Religious*, 1987, 46, 831–843.

[14]*Agent*, 221.

[15]*Spiritual Exercises, op. cit.*, 316.

[16]Josef Sudbrack, "Unterscheidung der Geister—Unterscheidung im Geiste," in Kurt Niederwimmer, Josef Sudbrack and Wilhelm Schmidt, *Unterscheidung der Geister: Skizzen zu einer neu zu lernenden Theologie des Heiligen Geistes*. Kassel: Johannes Stauda Verlag, 1972, 48.

[17]*The Letters of William James*, ed. Henry James. Boston: The Atlantic Monthly Press, 1920, 1:199. Quoted in Erik H. Erikson, *Identity, Youth and Crisis*. New York: Norton, 1968, 19. Italics as in Erikson.

[18]*The Autobiography of St. Ignatius Loyola, op. cit.*, 37.

[19]Cf. *Spiritual Exercises, op. cit.*, no. 172.

[20]The Latin version is: "Haec prima sit agendorum regula: sic Deo fide, quasi rerum successus omnis a te, nihil a Deo penderet; ita tamen iis operam omnem admove, quasi tu nihil, Deus omnia solus sit facturus." It can be found in "Selectae S. Patris nostri Ignatii Sententiae," no. II, in *Thesaurus Spiritualis Societatis Jesu*. Roma: Typis Polyglottis Vaticanis, 1948, 480. Gaston Fessard, in a long appendix to volume I of his *La Dialectique des Exercices Spirituels de Saint Ignace de Loyola* (Paris: Aubier, 1966), traces the historical background of the saying. He demonstrates that although not from Ignatius' own hand the saying does express the dialectic of his spirituality.

[21]In *The Transformation of Man* (Springfield, IL: Templegate Publishers, 1980) Rosemary Haughton makes a very useful distinction between formation structures (which, for her, are the same as secular structures) and transformation or conversion struc-

tures. The former try to set up the conditions that make the latter more possible. In terms of the question of community the formation structures are those rules of meeting and ways of conversing that make it more possible that the conversion to authentic community may occur.

[22]In *Let This Mind Be in You: The Quest for Identity Through Oedipus to Christ* (Minneapolis: Winston, 1985) Sebastian Moore argues cogently that it is the "voice" of original sin which whispers to us that the way things are is the way they have to be.

[23]Rosemary Haughton, *The Passionate God.* London: Darton, Longman and Todd, 1982, 2–3.

7. A Theology of the Ministry of Spiritual Direction

[1]*The Spiritual Exercises of St. Ignatius, op. cit.*, nn. 230–231. We might note that Ignatius' principle about love showing itself in deeds can be seen as an older version of the modern liberation theology's idea that orthopraxis reveals or is a test of orthodoxy.

[2]*Ibid.*, n. 234.

[3]Smith, *Experience and God, op. cit.*, 159–160.

[4]*Practice,* op. cit., 11.

[5]In *Mentoring: The Ministry of Spiritual Kinship* (Notre Dame, IN: Ave Maria, 1990) Edward Sellner notes that the Irish *anamchara* or soul friend is a descendant of the kind of spiritual mentoring developed among the desert fathers and mothers. The Irish tradition not only affected the development of the sacrament of penance in the western church, "but also, as noted spiritual theologians Jean Leclerq and Louis Bouyer acknowledge, the whole growth of Christian spirituality. According to Leclerq and Bouyer, this ministry affirmed 'a feeling in man that his relations with God can take the form of effective dialogue,' and because of that conviction all of Christian spirituality has been transformed." (62–63)

[6]Cf. William A. Barry, *"Now Choose Life:" Conversion as the Way to Life*. New York/Mahwah: Paulist, 1990.

[7]Smith, *op. cit.*, 163.

[8]*Ibid.*, 163.

[9]*Op. cit.*, 121.

[10]Eugene C. Kennedy and Vincent J. Heckler, *The Catholic Priest in the United States: Psychological Investigations*. Washington, DC: United States Catholic Conference, 1972, 9–11.

[11]Cf. Barry and Connolly, *Practice*, chapter 8, for a discussion of the traits desirable in a competent spiritual director.

[12]J. D. Salinger, *Franny and Zooey*. Toronto, New York: Bantam Books, 1964, 109.

[13]Sellner, *op. cit.*, 68.

[14]For a development of the notions of the working alliance and of transference and countertransference and their application to spiritual direction cf. Barry and Connolly, *op. cit.*, chapters 9 and 10.

[15]*Ibid.*, chapter 11. For the distinction between supervision and consultation cf. William A. Barry, "Supervision Improves Ministry," *Human Development*, 9/1 (1988), 27–30.

[16]Susan Howatch, *Glittering Images, op. cit.*, 171–172.

[17]One source of names of spiritual directors is the new group Spiritual Directors International whose central office is presently located at 2300 Adeline Drive, Burlingame, CA 94010. One can also contact some of the many training centers for spiritual directors.

[18]Again, to find the names of potential supervisors in a particular area, one could contact Spiritual Directors International or one of the training centers, as mentioned in previous note.

8. Conclusion

[1]*Anselm of Canterbury. Volume I.* Ed. and tr. by Jaspar Hopkins and Herbert Richardson. Toronto and New York: Edwin Mellen Press, 1974, 92.

[2]Ignatius of Loyola, *The Spiritual Diary,* n. 48. In *Ignatius of Loyola: The Spiritual Exercises and Selected Works.* Ed. George E. Ganss, S.J. New York/Mahwah: Paulist, 1991, 244–245.